Heather and gorse at Walton Heath

Golf in the Heather and Gorse

by David Worley

First Published 2015 by David Worley
PO Box 2063, Brighton 3186, Australia
Tel: (+61) 3 9596 6751
Email: where2playgolf@bigpond.com.au
www.golfbooks.com.au
Purchase enquiries may be directed to the above

© David Worley
Worley, David 1945-
Golf in the Heather and Gorse
ISBN: 978-0-9577527-3-3

Also written and published by David Worley:
Bill Edgar – A Legend in Amateur Golf
Fairways in Heaven, Bunkers from Hell
Journey through the Links
Another Journey through the Links

Designed by Graphic Partners
Melbourne Australia
www.graphicpartners.com.au

Printed in China through The Australian Book Connection

Front cover photo: St George's Hill
Back cover photo: The Berkshire – Blue Course

CONTENTS

This book is dedicated to my dear golfing friend from Glasgow,
Duncan Martin,
who died February 7th, 2015

FOREWORD
BY PETER THOMSON

David Worley is the envy of all of us who spend our wanderings seeking out spectacular courses on which to try our skills at golf. The game affords us perhaps endless opportunity to indulge our passions just as our photographer come author has followed his particular bliss. He has offered us the thrill and fascination of finding the classically popular in these pages. It brings back memories to those amongst who have done battle over these courses such as Walton Heath, Wentworth, Sunningdale and dozens more. I remember immediately spending a full day jousting with Arnold Palmer over Wentworth's "Burma Road", one summer's day when 36 holes and wooden heads were the norm. Walton Heath too was the scene of an almost perpetual Match Play Championship during high dry summers. These courses made history just as the golfers did. And like the clubhouses, understated and modest mostly that added to the charm and dignity and precious recall. Golf up and down Britain is a feature of its sporting treasures, open to all, if only through the camera lens. Is it matched anywhere else? I doubt it.

Worley has a unique way of presenting inland golf as an art form. The game is played in Nature's own garden as this book records, and since the glimpse we are offered in these pages represent the wide scope of sporting landscape, it offers for our judgement the best of inland golf. There are any number of seaside links books to fill our libraries which claim the high ground. Which is better? Do we need to answer the questions?

Here is a comprehensive collection of illustrated gems of natural golf perfectly illustrated and texted for our education. It is a precious document that shows off Britain's treasures of the game of golf. Worley's wander lust has favoured us with an inside picture of the multitude of golf courses that make up the whole fabric. Oh! To wander thither and take our clubs with us. Pleasure awaits.

Peter Thomson

Peter Thomson and the author at Sorrento Golf Club, April 2015

Swinley Forest

INTRODUCTION

Lee Trevino is purported to have said: "If Heaven is as good as this I hope they have some tee times left". I have been fortunate to play many courses in Britain where those exact sentiments were forefront in my mind.

Having previously written extensively about virtually every links course in the Kingdom and Ireland I wanted to complete the picture by playing, photographing and writing about my experiences on some of the best inland and heathland tracks in England and Scotland.

The definitive term 'inland' is perhaps a little misleading. Perhaps a better definition of the courses in this book would be to simply describe them as 'non links'. The golf courses I have included are a combination of heathland and parkland and in some cases are almost right at the edge of the sea. North Berwick East (sometimes known as The Glen), Longniddry, Stranraer, Carradale and Portpatrick are all on or very near the Scottish coastline but, mainly due to their soil, are not links. Similarly in England with East Devon, Isle of Purbeck and Carlyon Bay there are sea views but none of these could be classified as a links course.

One of my favourite holiday places in Scotland is the lovely Isle of Arran which lies off the west coast between Ayr and the Mull of Kintyre. Here there are no less than 7 golf courses and I have added the best four of these into this book. I have used 'writer's prerogative' and included Shiskine. Yes, I know Shiskine is most definitely a links, and a very good one at that, but it was omitted from my books on links courses[1] purely because it was only 12 holes. And I could not revue the best courses on Arran and not include Shiskine.

There is so much variety and natural beauty, particularly at the heathland courses, whether it be stands of Scots Pines, rows of birches, blooming rhododendrons, flowering broom and gorse and flanks of pink and purple heather. The majesty of James Braid's wonderful creation at Gleneagles, the breathtaking views from Strathpeffer Spa, the quaintness of Boat of Garten, the picturesque Loch Lomond, the quirky charm of Windermere, and the magnificent cluster of heathland gems especially in the Surrey area – this is golf at its finest.

I defer from ranking courses in any set numerical order but I do critique them in an honest and objective manner and if there are genuine shortcomings then they are not ignored from my summations.

The time available to you will naturally have a major influence on the destinations you choose.

As has been my practice in the past, the various courses are more or less set out in a geographic order that you might consider as the basis for your planning. Scotland begins in the southeast and then inland, north to the highlands and finally the west coast. The Isle of Arran, often thought of as Scotland in miniature, is given a specific chapter.

The journey through England starts from the Lake District in the north and continues down the central spine to within a few miles of London. It is really quite extraordinary just how many world class courses are in the heathland belt just 25 miles or so from London. From there it is due west and the delights of Dorset, Devon and Cornwall.

I am sure you will be able to use my book as a valuable golf/travel resource to experience many of these courses and to hopefully have memorable days that often result in new friendships.

---

[1] *"Journey through the Links", David Worley, 2007. "Another Journey through the Links", David Worley, 2010.*

Sunningdale in late afternoon

SCOTLAND

1. North Berwick East
   – The Glen
2. Longniddry
3. Glenbervie
4. Ladybank
5. Kingarrock
6. Forfar
7. Edzell
8. Downfield
9. Gleneagles
   – Kings
   – Queens
10. Auchterarder
11. Blairgowrie
    – Rosemount
12. Pitlochry
13. Strathpeffer Spa
14. Elgin
15. Grantown-on-Spey
16. Boat of Garten
17. Spey Valley
18. Ballater
19. Balmoral
20. Braemar
21. Dunblane New
22. Callander
23. Loch Lomond
24. The Carrick
25. Carradale
26. Belleisle
27. Stranraer
28. Portpatrick
29. Brodick
30. Lamlash
31. Whiting Bay
32. Shiskine

ENGLAND

33. Windermere
34. Pannal
35. Alwoodley
36. Moortown
37. Cavendish
38. Lindrick
39. Notts
40. Sherwood Forest
41. Woodhall Spa
    – Hotchkin
42. Beau Desert
43. Little Aston
44. Woburn
    – Dukes
    – Duchess
45. Ashridge
46. Berkhamsted
47. The Berkshire
    – Red
    – Blue
48. Royal Ashdown Forest
49. Sunningdale
    – Old
    – New
50. St George's Hill
51. Hankley Common
52. West Hill
53. Worplesdon
54. Woking
55. New Zealand
56. Liphook
57. West Sussex
58. Wentworth
    – West
59. The Addington
60. Swinley Forest
61. Walton Heath
    – Old
    – New
62. Reigate Heath
63. Ferndown
64. Broadstone
65. Parkstone
66. Isle of Purbeck
67. East Devon
68. China Fleet
69. St Mellion
    – Nicklaus
    – Kernow
70. Carlyon Bay
71. Tehidy Park

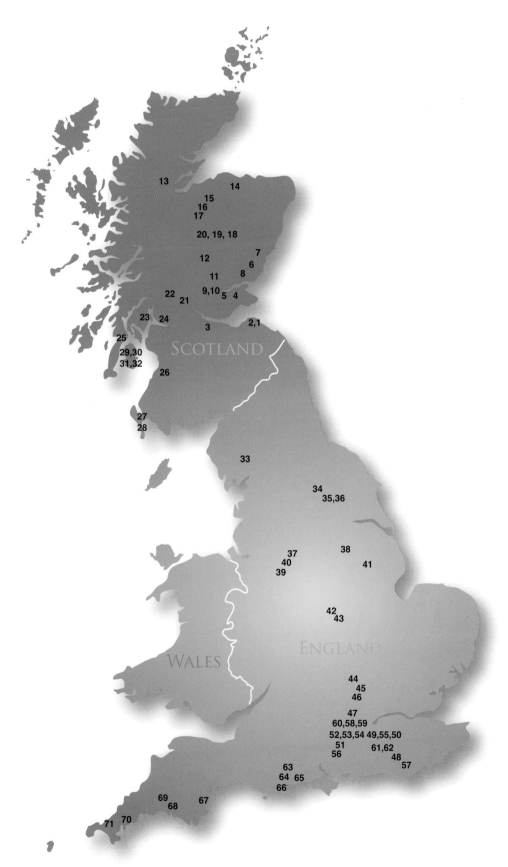

Above: North Berwick East and Craigleath
Below: Looking across the practice fairway and course to Bass Rock and its millions of gannets

SCOTLAND

Since 1996 I have undertaken eight lengthy golfing trips throughout Scotland and I have also driven around the complete coastline more than once with the exception of the very northwest tip where there is just the one golf course – Durness. Although this 9 holer has spectacular views, I could never justify the extra time for such a long trip with no guarantee of half decent weather for golf or photos. What I love about Scotland is the diversity and close proximity of courses virtually everywhere except for the mountainous northwest. Compared to England I also find that the minor roads are not so winding and it never takes long to venture from one destination to the next even though you may be in lovely quiet countryside.

Our journey commences on the south east of Scotland starting out at the very under-rated and frequently overlooked **North Berwick East**, also known as The Glen. Whilst the more famous North Berwick West links is one of my favourite places to golf in Scotland, I will readily concede that I should have spent more time exploring the delights of the East.

North Berwick is a lovely seaside harbour, just a short journey south of Edinburgh. The drive is along the A1 and then the coastal A198 passed the hallowed golfing village of Gullane where from the 7th tee of Gullane No 1 you can see no less than eight golf courses, including Muirfield.

As the name implies, the East Course is at the other end of town and occupies a spectacular piece of cliff-top land. The soil is of the heavier variety so this is not a links course like its neighbour on the west side of North Berwick. Whilst golf has probably been played in this area for several centuries, the East Course did not become 18 holes until 1906. Design is attributed to James Braid and Ben Sayers who was the legendary local professional and who has the amazing record of having played in 43 consecutive Open championships from 1880 to 1923.

The first hole leads you up to the cliff-top plateau where the views of the Firth of Forth and Bass Rock never cease to inspire. At the 4th, the first of the short holes you need to stay on the right hand side of the green to avoid a treacherous down hill putt. The par 5, 6th presents a challenge with out of bounds on the right. If you brought your camera then the 7th is the most elevated part of the course. At the long par 4, 8th(425 yards) you play toward the water and at the short 9th the green is right alongside the edge of the cliff. Disaster is never far away if you hook at the long par 4, 12th which is followed by one of the best par 3's in Scotland.

The 13th, 'Sea Hole' is a mere 148 yards downhill to the green. But beware as the tee shot is partly blind and the green is bordered by rocks and sand on two sides. Depending on wind direction you could be playing anything from a 4 iron to a 9 iron. Trouble lurks on the right of the 14th and 15th with the latter also featuring nine bunkers. After the challenge of OOB on the right of the 17th you finish with a drive from an elevated tee to the green below and the town as the backdrop.

Above: 13th green at low tide
Below: The 18th at North Berwick East
(Photos courtesy Ian Gust)

The wind can make North Berwick East very tricky but on a half decent day you are going to enjoy the course and the friendly environment in the clubhouse.

Heading back a little north and just inland from Aberlady Bay is the delightful **Longniddry**. Although you can see the sea from almost anywhere on the course the fairways are more of an inland variety and in some parts the trees are plentiful. A few of the more open holes such as the par 3, 4th have a links feel that is further enhanced with the presence of pot bunkers.

Above: The par 3, 4th has a distinct links feel
Below: 5th and 6th greens at Longniddry
(Photos courtesy Longniddry GC / Glyn Satterley)

You are bound to enjoy the 5th, a mischievous short dog-leg par 4 of 310 yards with a severely tiered and raised green. I wonder how many golfers playing here for the first time have had their first putt from the front of the green roll right back to their feet.

Some of the holes up to the 11th are lined by trees and holes 11 to 15 are the closest to the sea. The 18th is an excellent finish – a

par 4 requiring the tee shot to carry over 100 yards to the fairway and the second to be played over a gully to the green in front of the stone clubhouse. While Longniddry is not long and has no par 5's, it has eight par 4's over 400 yards and can be a testing par 68. It has in the past been used as a qualifying course for the Open but now would be considered too short.

You can't find much better credentials than its original design in 1921 being the work of Harry Colt. Subsequent alterations have come from Braid, Mackenzie Ross and Donald Steel.

Heading north towards Stirling and bypassing Edinburgh you need to link up to the M9 and then detour near the town of Dunipace to **Glenbervie** Golf Club. Glenbervie is a good parkland course that drains well and provides lovely views of the distant Ochil Hills.

Above: Glenbervie's 368 yard finishing hole (Photo courtesy Glenbervie GC)
Below: Ladybank is a delightful semi heathland course with beautiful surrounds and excellent fairways and greens

Designed by the ubiquitous James Braid it opened in 1932 and in the past was used for regional qualifying for the Open. There are some good holes including several testing par 3's.

The par 4, 6th is one of the best. It is about 400 yards but, being uphill, plays considerably longer. A good drive is required to avoid bunkers left and thick rough to the right. You then have to avoid trees to reach the undulating green. Index 1 is the 9th, a long dog-leg par 4 with OOB along the right. Bluebells are in abundance here in spring. Another good hole is the 14th, a longish par 4, slightly uphill to a sloping green below the clubhouse. If you are playing Glenbervie in spring then make sure you have your camera for the rhododendrons near the 17th green.

The well treed par 4, 18th climbs back to the welcoming clubhouse which overlooks most of the course. Glenbervie is parkland but with its mature trees and scenery it is well worth a game.

Moving further north you have the option of either the A91 or the A92 in the direction of St Andrews as you head to **Ladybank**, a few miles beyond the town of Glenrothes. Golf was first played here on an organized basis in 1879 when Old Tom Morris designed 6 holes.

The golf course is very much hidden away in the countryside just off the B9129 but is well signposted. Ladybank is a charming inland course with a heathland feel as you play amongst the pines and birches. It is challenging without being too difficult and it is easy walking but is never monotonous or uninteresting. To me it is such a pity that so many travellers to St Andrews miss out on this little gem.

The lovely tree lined 17th at Ladybank

LADYBANK
Golf Club

17

Beeches

**391
YARDS
PAR 4
S.I. 16**

The course can be lengthened by a few hundred yards which has helped it in on seven occasions to host qualifying when the Open is at St Andrews. There are a number of dog-legs which put a premium on accuracy from the tee. The 3rd bends right whilst the 9th, Index 1, turns left with a large tree guarding the corner. The 14th is straight ahead but it is a demanding par 4 of 462 yards to an undulating green. The 15th bends right but at the lovely 16th there is a sharp 60 degrees turn to the left.

The 17th runs fairly straight through a spectacular line of trees with one of the entrance roads along the right hand side. The 18th is the only hole requiring any sort of carry off the tee as you drive over grassy banks and hollows from an old quarry.

There are two entrances to the club. On one of them you enter from a short road into the car park. Try for the charming longer entrance road (off the B9129) that runs for some distance through a forested area and eventually alongside the 17th and 18th holes.

Ladybank's 18th from the tee

I'm not sure how I first heard about **Kingarrock** but once I was aware of it then it was a must experience golfing destination. It is located about 10 miles west of St Andrews just off the A91 at Hill of Tarvit near the town of Cupar.

A 9 hole golf course that first existed around 1924 on this magnificent estate of the Sharp family was recently restored with the help of the National Trust and the R & A.

The house is open to visitors and includes a lovely little café that I can recommend for lunch or afternoon tea. The pretty grounds include croquet fields, one of which was once a beautifully manicured grass tennis court.

The house overlooks the pretty 9 hole course that is maintained by a staff of just one – by chance an Australian expat who did his apprenticeship twenty

Above: par 3, 2nd Kingarrock
Below: looking back to what was the Sharp family home and gardens

years ago at the renowned Kingston Heath near Melbourne.

As an experiment, for the next two years they will not be using any artificial fertilizers or weed killer.

You can only play Kingarrock with the old hickory clubs that you select. Balls and 'reddy tees' are provided. The golf balls have been specifically made so as to approximate the distance you would achieve with a ball circa 1924 or 1898 – your choice. (1898 was the year the Haskell ball was patented as the first rubber wound golf ball.)

Our host was the charming David Anderson who took great pleasure in explaining the history of Kingarrock. If you play your cards right then your round will be rewarded with a wee nip at the conclusion. Make sure he shows you the copy of the original rules of golf as set out on the 7th March 1744.

As a young boy of about ten I learned to play golf with a small set of cut down ladies hickory clubs so I was keen to relive that memory. To my surprise it took me at least 4 holes before I could come to terms with judging flight and distance, especially with the modified balls. It did not help that the rough was unusually long and thick due to the cool summer in 2014.

The holes are relatively undulating and the greens are understandably quite small. Time did not allow us to play a second 9 which I strongly recommend as you will need much of your first sortee round the course to get familiar with your equipment. There are only a few shallow bunkers but all are made a bit more difficult by the long grassy 'eyebrows'.

I am sure you will enjoy the fun and relative solitude of Kingarrock and its unique ambience. Don't take the golf too seriously.

Above: 5th green
Below: Our charming host at Kingarrock, David Anderson

The A92 crosses the Tay Bridge and heads north as the A90. The course at **Forfar** in Angus is located on the A932. Initially laid out by Old Tom Morris in 1871, alterations were made in 1926 by James Braid. This is another pretty location enhanced by the many Scots Pines and views to the Angus Glens. Some interesting fairway stances are the result of the remnants of old furrows on the fairways that date back to when flax was grown here.

There are a few bends left (3rd hole) and right (4th and 7th holes) but mostly it is straight ahead through the pines. There are some well bunkered holes – the par 3, 5th has five greenside bunkers, the

Above: Undulating fairway on the 10th at Forfar
Below: The well bunkered 8th hole
(Photos courtesy Forfar GC)

A burn is very much in play at the par 3, 9th (Photo courtesy Forfar GC)

par 4, 6th has four to catch the drive, the 8th has four fairway and three greenside hazards, the short par 5, 14th has no less than seven in the last 130 yards and the par 4, 17th contains three bunkers in play for the tee shot and another four for the approach.

Most of the hazards are at the front of the greens so it is generally better to be long rather than short. Surprisingly there are few burns with the one such danger spot being just left of the green at the short 9th.

The journey continues north along the A90 before turning left at the B966 to **Edzell**. The golf club is located right beside the village, in the foothills of the Grampians, and dates back to 1895.

The holes vary nicely in terms of length and there are a number of cross-bunkers. The par 4, 2nd, is a stiff test at 447 yards into the prevailing wind and with OOB on the right. The 3rd, a short par 4 of only 311 yards, can be a real chance of birdie but the approach is well bunkered and the green is two-tiered.

There are attractive aspects to the 5th, 7th, 8th and 9th holes with the latter following the course of the river. The 10th features cross-bunkers and a slightly plateaued green followed by a par 4 of 444 yards with a narrow tree lined fairway.

By the time you have finished the 13th, another long par 4, you are looking for some respite as the only par 3 so far has been at the 189 yard 6th.

Par 4, 15th at Edzell (Photo courtesy Edzell GC)

At last there is a short hole, the 14th - uphill and with a well protected green. The 15th is one of the prettiest at Edzell. It is a fairly short par 4 but you need to avoid the old railway track on the left and the OOB and thick line of Scots pines along the right. There are also cross-bunkers towards the green.

At the 16th you play your approach to a very elevated green and then at the 17th you are on the highest tee of the course where there are great views of the surrounding countryside. The par 5 closing hole is enhanced by the lovely setting of the village directly behind the clubhouse.

From Edzell it is south, down the A92 to **Downfield** which is about two miles north of Dundee. Check your directions carefully as Downfield can be a little hard to find. You need to look for the A923 and then Turnberry Avenue.

Downfield was the venue for the very first Scottish open in 1972. It features magnificent stands of conifers on almost every hole so any stray shots will leave you chipping out from under the trees. There are also water hazards on no less than seven holes. When I last visited Downfield it had been at the end of one of the wettest June months on record so the course was playing quite long. It measures 6817 yards from the white tees and is par 73 with five par 5's. It can be harder to score off the blue tees as the 7th, 11th and 13th are reduced to par 4's.

11th green (Photo courtesy Downfield GC)

Much of Downfield is picture-postcard, but none more so than the 11th green and the par 3, 12th known as Davy Jones' Locker, which apparently was a favourite hole of Gary Player. The water hazard here is scenic but does not really come into play unless you duff your tee shot or hit a huge slice. The 14th is an excellent dogleg par 5 with thick trees on the left and a burn along most of the right hand side.

I always enjoy short but tricky par 4's, so the 16th is one to challenge you. It plays downhill to a sharp right-angled bend. You must stay on the middle of the fairway and it is essential not to finish shorter than about 270 yards off the tee, otherwise you will be looking at the lovely tall pine trees between your ball and the invitingly close green. Downfield finishes with another good tree-lined dogleg at the 18th.

The A90 and then the A9 heading southwest is a pleasant drive through the peaceful town of Perth and then on towards Auchterarder and the magnificent hotel and golf courses at **Gleneagles**.

Above: Downfield's 18th and its magnificent tree-lined fairways (Photo courtesy Downfield GC)
Below: Gleneagles Hotel as seen from the King's Course

Apart from the Wee Course (9 par 3's), there are three courses at Gleneagles. The King's and Queen's are two of James Braid's finest creations. The more recent Jack Nicklaus designed PGA Centenary (formerly known as The Monarchs) features cart paths and is definitely not on my play list even though it was the venue for the 2014 Ryder Cup.

Above:The 1st green on the King's has a surprising amount of slope
Below: 10 bunkers protect the green on the par 4,14th, Dainty Den

Approaching the 17th green and looking down the par 4, 18th at Gleneagles King's Course

It is often stated that the Queen's is the more picturesque. I would beg to differ – I feel that the King's is the better in terms of quality and scenery and is certainly more challenging as the Queen's is somewhat shorter.

The first hole on the **King's Course** sets the scene – deceptively more difficult than it appears with its wide fairway. The shot to the green must be perfect as the slope can make for 3 putts if you are above the hole. The par 4, 2nd is downhill and the view from half way along the fairway is one of absolute peace and tranquility across the valley below. The sign on the 3rd tee should read "welcome to the gorse". The drive is through a gap in the gorse and then you must hit blind over a steep hill to a hidden two-tiered green. I know Mike Clayton[1] hates this hole.

The elevated green at the short 5th will add some fear and trepidation to the lesser golfer – there is no bailout area here just very steep slopes all round and four bunkers at the front. The 6th is a par 5 from the white tees but from the yellow it is shortened by just 21 yards but it becomes a tough par 4. Be careful at the 7th not to take on too much of the corner at the dogleg.

The 13th is Braid's signature hole. It is a par 4 of 464 yards but does not play that long. The very recognizable 14th (Dainty Den) is a par 4 of 260 yards from the white tees (309 from the very back tees) that is driveable, even for me, but there are ten bunkers to negotiate. The one just short and left of the green is a frequent attraction to many golfers.

As you walk to the 15th tee look to your left at the picture-perfect view of the hotel framed between the pine trees. The par 3,16th (Wee Bogle) is challenging with a green that slopes from the back and surrounded by nine bunkers. Don't be fooled by it being rated the easiest hole. At the 17th you need two accurate draw shots. Many lost balls finish up in the grassy banks on the left of this hole.

Gleneagles King's is golf on a grand scale and the 18th is an appropriate finish from an elevated tee with the Grampians in the distance. Make sure you avoid the nasty pot bunkers with your drive.

I have played the King's on a number of occasions and it will always be high on my list of favourite golfing experiences. By good fortune I seem to always enjoy fine weather when I visit Gleneagles. Having played the King's on three different trips I was eager to try the Queen's Course. **Gleneagles Queen's** was a very enjoyable round of golf but I would not rate it as anywhere near as good as the King's even though the day I played the Queen's it was the warmest I have experienced there and conditions were perfect.

The opening is a good par 4 of 409 yards, uphill and bending slightly to the left. This is followed by a fairly lacklustre par 3 with a plateau green. The fourth can be a short par 4 if you manage to get your drive over the ridge. The fifth is an excellent well-bunkered short hole of 177 yards and the sixth is a good par 4 of 437 yards from the white tees.

---

[1] *Mike Clayton was a successful professional golfer on the Australian and European tour before commencing his Golf Architecture business, now in conjuction with Geoff Ogilvy.*

Above: The 6th at the Queen's Course is a good par 4 of 437 yards
Below: Anything right is probably lost ball at the 15th

An obvious weakness of the Queen's is its lack of length. The 7th is the only par 5 for men (there are six for the ladies) and it is a mere 491 yards from the normal tees. At the 9th you need a straight drive to the corner of the 90 degree dog-leg right and then the fairway runs steeply uphill.

Caution is required at the par 4, 10th as you near the green. About 100 yards out the fairway is very narrow and turns hard left with thick rough on both sides. The 13th is not a difficult par 3 provided you are not short left (long grass) or too far right where there is a large pond near the green. Another par 3 follows at the 14th. It plays longer than its 215 yards and is uphill to a steeply sloping two- tiered green.

The short par 4 at the 15th is a possible card wrecker even though it is only 252 yards in length. The fairway runs uphill and slopes severely to the thick grass and bracken on the right. The two fairway bunkers are well placed and are hard to avoid. An accurate drive is essential at the 16th and then at the 17th there is yet another par 3. It is an attractive looking hole of 204 yards to a long and narrow green. This is not the place to be wide with your tee shot.

The 18th is one of the best – a par 4 from high up where you hit over a marshy pond and ravine. Keep your drive slightly right of center for a straight shot into the green. Anything too far left will be blocked out by trees.

The front nine holes is the longer of the two. The back nine is lacking with three par 3's and a short par 4 from holes thirteen to seventeen. The greens and fairways are always very good at Gleneagles and the Queen's was fun to play notwithstanding its shortcomings.

Above: Accuracy is needed at the par 3, 17th
Below: The par 4, 18th is one of the best holes on the Queen's Course

From the Queens there are some good views of the new David McLay Kidd course that was supposed be ready for play in 2013. (I can't find any information to indicate it was ever completed or is open for play). The al-Tajir family (owners of the Highland Springs bottled water business) made an offer to buy the Gleneagles complex but were rejected so they decided to build their own hotel and golf course. Kidd's father was the greenkeeper at Gleneagles so this is land that the designer knows well. From what I saw it is similar land to that of the Kings but there are not nearly as many trees.

The nearby town of **Auchterarder** is pretty much one long high street and the golf course is in full view if you are approaching from the Gleneagles hotel direction. Auchterarder is short at only 5775 yards but it is in a very pretty setting and some of the six par 3's are quite challenging. There are some gentle hills and surprisingly there are 3 par 5's. Where it is lacking is that only one par 4 (the 17th) is of any real length at 441 yards.

The first tee shot will get your attention as you must drive over a stone wall and avoid the large tree to the right. The 6th is a very short par 5 at only 473 yards but it plays uphill with trees all along the right and gets a rating as the hardest hole.

Above: 9th green and the pretty views at Auchterarder
Below: The long par 3, 14th (Photo courtesy Auchterarder GC)

The par 3, 8th is an interesting one shotter where you are well and truly among the tall pines. The 11th is a birdie chance being only 331 yards in length but be wary of the wet ditch that runs all along the left. The 13th is a pretty hole appropriately named Ochil View – it is a short par 4, downhill, and represents another birdie chance before some more testing holes.

The par 3, 14th requires a semi-blind tee shot of 203 yards to a narrow green. At the par 5,15th watch for a large hollow just in front of the green. You then encounter the difficult 16th, a par 3 of 235 yards followed by the long par 4, 17th rated Index number 2.

The hole I always remember is the par 3, 18th which runs 184 yards slightly uphill. A pretty two-storey house is only about 30 yards behind the green and is protected by a low stone and hedge fence. The hole plays a little longer than it looks but for a first time visitor you can't help thinking about the close proximity of the house.

Pick a nice day and you will enjoy the tranquility, good views and some interesting holes at Auchterarder.

Auchterarder Golf Club is a lovely tranquil setting

We are now heading north and next golfing stop is along the A93 to Blairgowrie. There are two 18 hole courses at **Blairgowrie** Golf club – the Rosemount and the Landsdowne. By far the elder statesman is the Rosemount, originally designed by Alister MacKenzie and later James Braid. In 1977 this was the scene of Greg Norman's first win on the European Tour. The Landsdowne is somewhat longer and tighter and opened as recently as 1979. If you get a chance you should at least have a look at the Wee Course – a wonderful mix of par 3's and short par 4's incorporating some of Dr. MacKenzie's original work.

I can never forget my first journey here way back in 1996 which was a very wet summer. We had booked lunch and golf on the Landsowne which was the only course available that day to visitors. We sat at a bay window in the charming upstairs lounge and watched the rain pour down for the whole day! The return trip in 1998 provided a lovely balmy day and my wife and I played the Rosemount with a former Captain of the Club. Not much seems to have changed when I recently revisited.

The **Rosemount** opens with a delightful par 4 of about 400 yards that is lined with trees on both sides. It is not an overly long course so accuracy can be well rewarded. Two of the par 5's become 4's off the visitors tees. At the 5th this means taking off 85 yards but at the 11th you gain only 34 yards so it is more difficult to match par when played as a 4. Whilst the fairway bunkers are relatively sparse they are well positioned, for example on holes seven, eleven, twelve and fourteen where it is essential they are avoided with your drive.

Blairgowrie's clubhouse and the 18th green, Rosemount Course (Photo courtesy Donald Ford Images)

Two of the very memorable holes are the 15th and 16th. At the short 15th (Wee Dunt) you can't really see all of the five greenside bunkers. The green falls away at the back and if you are not accurate off the tee then there are thick trees to the left and a pond far right. The 16th tee is a lovely peaceful location where you first must drive over the pond before negotiating a tight second shot on this testing par 4. The fairway bends left and is 473 yards from the back tees and still 435 yards from the forward tees. This is definitely the hardest hole on the Rosemount. From the green there are picturesque views along the short 17th.

The par 3, 17th at Blairgowrie is one of the best short holes in Scotland

16th tee – 'Black Loch' (Photo courtesy Donald Ford Images)

The penultimate hole is rightly regarded as one of the best par 3's in Scotland. The 17th is only 163 yards slightly uphill but there are two bunkers at the front right, another at the left and a devilish sloping, split-level green among the birches. The burn that crosses the fairway half way to the green should not be in play. The round concludes with a fabulous par 4 as you play towards the character filled clubhouse. There are birch trees left of the green and heather is at the right.

You are hard to please if you don't enjoy your golf at Blairgowrie which is certainly one of the best inland layouts in Scotland.

Driving north to Pitlochry you have the option of the A93 and then the A924 or the A923 to near Dunkeld and on to the A9. Distance wise there is not much difference but my experiences in Scotland have taught me that unless you prefer a longer, and maybe more scenic, drive then it is always better to use the major roads wherever possible so I suggest you head for the A9.

Pitlochry is one of the prettiest courses in Scotland and from high up there are wide views down the Tummel Valley. The layout is hilly and this can be a wet area so try for some dry conditions if you can. Pitlochry was initially laid out in 1908 by Willie Fernie of Troon. The total length is a modest 5700 yards (par 69 for men) but the slopes, tight tree-lined fairways, burns and well bunkered greens make this a good challenge. Whilst there are no par 5's (there are three for the ladies), this is offset to some extent by having only three par 3's.

Don't be put off by the climb of the first few holes that seem to meander endlessly uphill. After three testing holes you play the first of the short holes located on the site of an ancient Pictish Fort. This is lovely countryside with the 5th green in a delightful setting of trees and shrubs.

6th green. The hole is named 'Druid Stones' because of the Pictish stone circle in the woods to the right of the fairway. (Photo courtesy Pitlochry GC)

Pitlochry's 12th hole (Photo courtesy Pitlochry GC)

At the par 4, 9th there are some great views across the course but don't let this distract you too much as there is OOB and trees on the left and then a fairly heavily bunkered approach area. The second of the short holes is the 185 yard 11th where you will encounter trees along the right and no less than six bunkers in front of the green. The par 4, 12th is downhill but is rated the second hardest at Pitlochry. The fairway narrows considerably from where you should be playing your second shot which must negotiate a burn about 60 yards in front of the putting surface.

The thirteenth is an excellent par 4 where you need to avoid the burn at the left for the tee shot and then the five bunkers when playing to the green. Two short par 4's of less than 300 yards follow. The club claims that the fifteenth, needing an accurate drive before approaching the small sloping green, is one of the most difficult par 4's of under 300 yards anywhere in the world. You be the judge.

You will easily remember the spectacular par 3, 16th measuring 180 yards. You hit downhill with OOB right, trees left and deep rough with six bunkers greenside. I really like the finishing hole. You might be tempted to open your shoulders as after all it is only 328 yards downhill. The reward is more than matched by the risks – OOB all down the right, pockets of trees on both sides and then a wide burn just in front of a green with three bunkers. The green setting near the clubhouse is charming as is the clubhouse itself.

There are a number of options as to what order you consider playing the eight courses in the highlands that I am reviewing. For simplicity I am suggesting we start with the northernmost and then gradually work south before heading to the west side of Scotland. This is a fairly long trip on the A9, past Inverness and then the A835 followed by a few miles on the A834 to Strathpeffer.

Looking across the course at Strathpeffer

Strathpeffer Spa Golf Club is the perfect starting point as it really does feel like you are at the top of the world above the amazing little town/village. Strathpeffer became a popular holiday spa town after the railway line was built in the mid 1880's. The closure of the line not long after the Second World War has meant that it has almost stopped in time and has preserved its quaint Swiss mountain village look. The station has been restored and now contains shops and craft exhibitions.

Strathpeffer has a unique charm

It is almost pointless to try to describe individual holes – you need to see this beautiful highland gem for yourself. The well regarded American golf course architect Tom Doak commented some years ago that you need a Sherpa at Strathpeffer Spa. It is very hilly but you can't just rate this course purely on its rather average architectural merits. The scenery is the best of any golf course in Scotland and it is so peaceful you will feel at one with nature as you play alongside the thick pine forest and over burns and ponds and contemplate the many blind shots necessitated by the hilly terrain.

The original nine holes were the work of Willie Park (Jnr) in 1888 but Old Tom Morris is credited with most of the eighteen hole design around the turn of the century.

The view from the first tee alone is breathtaking. To your right you can see for miles down the Peffery Valley and ahead it is the largest fall from tee to green of any course in the country. The hole measures just 330 yards but you need a solid drive to carry the burn and there is plenty of trouble by way of rough and trees near the green.

From the third to the sixth are all par 3's with three of them being quite long. The views everywhere are just sensational, particularly from the eighth and tenth tees. The short 10th plays across a pond to a small saucer green. At the short par 4,12th you play steeply downhill to what appears to be a very tiny green. I guess after a while you can judge the distances on these shots that are down big drops in the fairway, but first time round the club selection can be tricky. The par 3, 14th is probably the only flat hole on the layout.

The closing hole is almost as beguiling as the first. Perched high up on the course you play to a green beside the clubhouse some 333 yards away but very driveable because of the steep slope. You will either need some luck, or local knowledge, as you must get your ball to follow the terrain with a strong fade and avoid the low stone wall that protects the clubhouse side of the green. The boundary fence runs all along the right and the green slopes severely.

Strathpeffer Spa is definitely worth a game just for the scenery. The minimal staff maintain the course well and the small greens are surprisingly good. You can also be

The amazing opening hole at Strathpeffer Spa

sure of a friendly Scottish welcome in the clubhouse. If you decide to walk it then take a light bag and only about six or seven clubs… and don't forget your camera.

Looking back from the 18th green. The tee is high up on the left

From Strathpeffer the adventure takes us across the Moray Firth heading east on the A9 and A96 to the town of Elgin. On your way it is worth stopping at the site of the Battle of Culloden just near Nairn Dunbar Golf Club. The site has been well preserved and you can't help but be moved as you stand amongst the areas marking the particular Scots clans who met their death at the hands of the English at Culloden Field.

The golf course at **Elgin** is just six miles from the sea. It is wooded parkland that at times has a heathland feel. There is plenty of gorse and fairways lined with silver birches add to the scenic beauty, and there are also some pretty tough holes. The club was formed in 1906 and has been 18 holes since 1924.

There are no less than eight par 4's over 400 yards with five being over 450 yards. This contributes to a healthy length from the back tees of 6449 yards, even though there is only one par 5, and a short one at that. The first, second, fourteenth and eighteenth are particularly daunting into the wind with Index 1 being the 464 yard par 4, 14th.

The first of the short holes is the pretty 4th -159 yards down a narrow fairway through birches to a plateau green. The 5th, the only par 5, is a mere 483 yards but is rated the second hardest at Elgin. The second shot is the difficulty being uphill to a landing area with a number of fairway and greenside bunkers.

Back to back par 3's at six and seven are followed by three demanding two-shotters each in excess of 400 yards. Whilst the twelfth is a potential birdie opportunity you need to look for the well disguised greenside bunkers. The par 3, 15th is an attractive hole played from elevated tee over an undulating grassy area that was formerly a quarry.

At the par 4, 17th you need to keep to the middle of the fairway to avoid being stymied by the big birch tree just short and right of the green. The final hole is a good finish to the round. Getting on in two is made all the more difficult as the green is at an angle and has a steep grassy bank on the right hand side. Elgin is usually well maintained and is a good test where you will need to play well to beat your handicap.

Southward bound, first on the A941 then the A95, will bring you within a mile or so of Grantown-on-Spey

16th green and the old water pump (Photos courtesy Elgin GC)

on the A939. This is a popular tourist location with other attractions such as fishing at the nearby Spey River, a number of whisky distilleries and the heritage Strathspey Railway.

Grantown-on-Spey Golf Club commenced in 1890 and both Willie Park and James Braid each had a hand in its development. Accuracy, not length, is paramount here. This is a holiday course of just 5710 yards but it is lots of fun in a beautiful location with magnificent pines and views of the Cromdale Hills in the Cairngorm range.

The 5th is the only par 5 at Elgin

The first six holes are on flat parkland terrain followed by six holes of moderately hilly woodland before the closing six holes of undulating parkland. A number of holes in the middle of the round have heathery sections, particularly the ninth and the twelfth. With the tightness of many of the tee shots the quietness here is often broken only by the sound of golf ball hitting timber.

I first visited Grantown-on-Spey many years ago primarily so I could experience the marvelous 9th – Murdie's View. The tee box is amongst the tall pines as you play downhill to a green 275 yards away. The fairway is lined first with heather and then a wall of pines. Beyond the green in the distance is the Cromdale Hills. Your chip to the green is just that little more difficult knowing that anything through the back will run down a very steep bank. On my most recent visit a fox accompanied me down the fairway.

This is also a rather wet part of Scotland so try to pick a dry day. On one summer's visit the Professional informed me that there had been some rain every day for the past 6 weeks - but it is worth the trip to just to see the 9th.

Just a few miles further south on the A95 is the village of Boat of Garten and the **Boat of Garten Golf** and Tennis Club with the Spey River on one side and the steam train line which runs to nearby Aviemore on the other. Every now and then you come across a golf course you feel like you could happily play endlessly. In my group of favourite links courses I have North Berwick West high on the list and among the inland courses the Boat is right up there. I'll go so far as to say if you don't enjoy and appreciate the Boat then you haven't understood how golf developed and you are taking this great game too seriously.

This is one of Braid's best with every hole different as you meander through the birches, heather and broom. Probably the only weakness is the par 3, 1st – a flat and featureless hole of 189 yards. From here

Murdie's View at Grantown-on-Spey

on keep it straight, expect some odd bounces from the bumpy fairways and enjoy the scenery and wonderful ambience where the only sound you will often hear is the steam train as it passes right behind the 3rd green on its way to Aviemore which is just a short trip but gives some lovely views across the course. Whilst on the train you could be forgiven for feeling as though you are in an Agatha Christie movie or perhaps the actor Kenneth More might come flying past in a green 1952 MG sports car.

The second hole immediately tells you what is in store. This lovely par 4 doglegs right with heather and birch trees waiting if you cut off too much of the bend. The par 3, 3rd plays over a valley to a saucer green with the railway line close behind at the rear. Any shot off line will be deflected even further in the wrong direction.

The first of the two par 5's is the fourth hole with its crumpled fairway and profuse heather and broom in front of the line of birches, particularly along the right. There are many very good holes but the sixth, 'Avenue', is one of the best. The fairway is quite narrow and it bends right to a green bunkered on both sides. The sloping fairway can be the danger at the seventh.

The second of the short holes is the ninth where you play slightly uphill and feel like you are surrounded by the birches. A hole I vividly remember from all of my trips is the narrow par 4, 12th, 'Craigellachie' with the imposing Cairngorms as the backdrop. A tricky double dog-leg par 5 is followed by lovely views of the Spey River from the fourteenth tee.

The short par 4,15th is a wonderfully quirky hole that is perhaps now a little easier than it appeared on my first adventure here. The drive is blind and there is a good chance you will be in the deep gully about half way to the green. This is now just light rough but previously it was full of thick heather which came as something of a shock

Above: Par 3, 3rd hole with the steam train behind
Below: Boat of Garten – broom, heather and birches

after you had driven blind down the middle of the fairway.

I would rate the long par 4, 18th as close to the hardest and it certainly can ruin a good score. The hole dog-legs right from the tee and then, provided you have found the fairway, you have a long second shot uphill to a very elevated green with thick trees all the way on the right for the approach.

The Boat is fun to play but it is not the place for wild hitters. I seem to recall Peter Thomson telling me some years ago that he had played there with the

The narrow 12th, 'Craigellachie'

The 18th green at Boat of Garten is a difficult target

The 15th, aptly named 'Gully'

Duke of York and they referred to it as 'the rifle range' in deference to the need for accuracy.

About five miles further south is the town of Aviemore and the new course owned by the Macdonald Hotel Group, **Spey Valley**. Designed by Dave Thomas, Spey Valley first opened for play in 2006. I played the course only a few years after it had opened so, although the fairways and greens were satisfactory, they still needed one more summer to thicken up. It will stretch even the longest hitters as the blue and white tees both provide a length in excess of 7000 yards. Even the most forward tees (yellow) are 6653 in length.

The first three holes, two par 4's and a par 5, are not too demanding and help get the field away without too much bother. But from the long par 3, 4th the degree of difficulty moves up a notch. You won't play many courses where there are four par 3's that average 210 yards.

The fifth is possibly the longest par 5 in Britain at 635 yards from the blue and even 608 from the yellow. From midway down the fairway there are lovely summer views of snow patches clinging to the Cairngorm Mountains. The scenic par 3, 6th has a small lake on the right that should not really be in play but the acres of heather certainly can be. The bunker right in front of the green is a popular finish for many tee shots.

At the seventh, a lovely downhill par 4, there are also huge areas of heather. The green is in a delightful setting with superb views across the course to the nearby mountains. The eighth is an unusual par 4 of 396 yards. It can be difficult first time here to know which way the fairway is heading. It dog-legs sharp left where there are two pine trees

Above: Spey Valley's 7th hole
Below: Keep to your right with the drive at the 9th

Par 3, 6th at Spey Valley

The dangerous par 3, 16th at Spey Valley

well out into the fairway. The left side is lined with heather and birch trees and then gorse as you get closer to the green.

At the 9th you play downhill and all the hazards are set out before you. This short two shotter of 330 yards is well bunkered. A lone pine is behind the first fairway bunker so you need to keep your drive just right of center. The par 3, 10th is straight forward provided you carry the heather. Eleven and twelve are brutally long par 4's but a potential card wrecker awaits you at the par 3, 16th.

From the back tee the 16th is 229 yards. You must carry two ponds with almost impenetrable heathery rough between them. Two bunkers guard the front right of the green and a smaller bunker is positioned left. The temptation is to over club which can leave you in the heather or the birch trees behind the green. Danger also lurks at the final hole where an accurate drive must avoid bunkers on the right and potential lost ball at the left near the River Spey.

Spey Valley was better than I had expected and should improve further as the course matures. Apart from being a long course, there are some lengthy walks from green to tee so you are advised to consider taking a cart (or buggy as they are called in the UK). The beautiful scenery is an added bonus to the golf.

The Cairngorm Mountains dictate that we must double back a few miles and then proceed south east along the A939 to **Ballater** near the junction with the A93. Ballater Golf Club dates back to 1892 and is situated in a beautiful part of Upper Deeside with several holes running close to the River Dee. It is an easy walking course with something of a heathland feel and the scenery is superb, as is the case with all of the courses with views of the Cairngorms in particular.

Ballater is well conditioned although I found the greens a little on the

Above: Par 3, 5th at Ballater
Below: An accurate drive is needed at the 11th at Ballater

slow side. It is not long at just 6059 yards but there are some rather tight holes and some very good par 3's the best of which is the 186 yard 5th. The hole demands an accurate tee shot and anything left will face a very tricky chip. The par 4, 4th (410 yards) is rated the most difficult. The tee is not far from the river. The fairway bends left and the green is raised so the second shot here is difficult.

The River Dee can also be in play on the left of the 6th and is dangerously close to the green at the short 13th. The final hole can be a dangerous short par 4 of just 328 yards. There is a wet ditch near the start of the fairway that also has three bunkers. A further three bunkers protect the green and OOB is very near the back left.

If you play off the yellow tees then the three par 5's become somewhat more difficult par 4's, particularly the seventh and eleventh holes.

With the broom and gorse in flower and surrounded by pine forests there is a lovely ambience here. Bunkers are well placed throughout the course but they are not very deep or demanding. Ballater is better than a holiday course but it is not overly challenging.

I played Ballater with a local, Alastair Carmichael, who kindly got permission for my wife and I to access the golf course in the Queen's grounds at Balmoral, located a few miles further west on the A93 near the village of Crathie.

Balmoral Golf Club is primarily only for those living nearby or workers on the estate. It is only nine holes but with alternate tees for eighteen holes. The clubhouse is a cute little timber hut given to the members by the Queen in 1995.

It is not a great golf course by any stretch of the imagination but the location is so lovely and quiet you are hard pressed not to enjoy yourself here. The greens are very small and the fairway turf is amazingly springy. While the rough may not have been long it was very lush and thick.

The quirky little par 3, 5th is only 125 yards in length but it is uphill and you have to hit through a ridiculously narrow gap in the tree canopy. Your best option may be for a low runner and bump it up the hill –but make sure you have enough elevation to clear the wet ditch in front of the ladies tee. At this end of the course there are lovely views of the house where the Prime Minister stays as do some members of the Royal Family, particularly for stays of a short duration. Some of the holes are very narrow and can also be fairly undulating, particularly the sixth, seventh and eighth.

My wife and I at the lovely little wooden clubhouse at Balmoral

7th hole

The 7th is a lovely downhill hole -the only par 5. The par 4, 8th 'Dairy Dip' is rated Index 1 and is a very tricky hole. It is not just narrow and undulating – it bends left and has OOB very much in play all down the left side as does the previous hole.

You will walk the eighteen holes in no time so enjoy a picnic lunch beside the 'clubhouse' and soak up the atmosphere – this is definitely nothing more than holiday golf but a wonderful experience if you get the chance to access the course.

A further five or six miles along the A93 is the very pretty village of Braemar located beside the River Clunie. The golf course at **Braemar** was built in 1903 and, at 1200 feet above seal level, is the highest eighteen holer in Scotland even though the course itself is flat and is in a valley amidst the Grampians.

Looking back down the tricky 8th at Balmoral

It is very short at only 4935 yards and, not surprisingly, there are no par 5's. There are however some challenging holes due to some burns, the River Clunie and a number of elevated greens.

The River Clunie runs through the course and is right behind the first green. At the tricky 369 yard par 4, 2nd the river runs all along the right, thick rough awaits you on the left and the green is quite elevated making the long second shot rather difficult.

With such a relatively flat course it is no surprise to find a number of burns as well as the river, for example, near the eighth and fifteenth greens. The fourth, tenth and fifteenth are par 4's in excess of 400 yards and are three of the more difficult holes at Braemar.

The last two holes are both par 3's but couldn't be more different. The penultimate hole is almost impossibly long at 245 yards with the river in front of the green. The 18th is only 122 yards but the green is forty feet above the tee and slopes from front to back.

2nd green and the River Clunie close by

Above: Looking across the course at Braemar
Below: The River Clunie runs right through the village and the golf course at Braemar

I recall being told by one of the locals that there are no bunkers at Braemar because they had become a nesting area for adders.

The Duke of York is the Patron at Braemar and, with Balmoral so nearby, is a frequent visitor. This is enjoyable holiday golf but I wouldn't fancy playing here after any sort of prolonged wet spell. There is a great little café situated right on the river in the village – you couldn't wish for a better setting for lunch.

This is the last of golf near the highlands so it is a longer trip through Perth once more

returning on the A9 to Dunblane heading towards Stirling.

Dunblane New was one of the very first courses I ever played in Scotland way back in 1996. I remember the experience vividly for two reasons. It was a freezing day in early May and I think I was wearing three jumpers. After the game we thawed out in the clubhouse and met Roy and Shirley Erskine who have had an amazing family history with the club. Roy is a past male Captain and Shirley has been the lady Captain. Their son Keith was a previous Club Champion and at that time was the professional at Irvine – a fine links course in Ayr. During afternoon tea with the Erskine's the topic changed to tennis which had been my great passion before succumbing to a shoulder injury. Their daughter was the Scottish national tennis coach and we later offered for the Erskine's teenage grandson to stay with us whilst he competed in the juniors at the Australian Open tennis in Melbourne. A last minute injury meant that he never made that trip – pity, and in case you haven't worked it out… it was Andy Murray.

One of the great delights in travelling around the country playing golf is that you meet so many wonderfully friendly people. We have remained friends with Roy and Shirley and try to catch up with them whenever we are in Scotland.

Dunblane New is a somewhat hilly parkland course with some lovely holes lined with birches and cherry blossoms. Many of the greens are set into the hillside slope so there is a real penalty if you miss on the low side. This is particularly evident at the seventh, ninth, fifteenth and sixteenth greens.

Top: Looking back to the 2nd tee
Middle: Par 3, 7th from behind
Bottom: The 9th dog-legs left to a severely plateaued green
(Photos courtesy Val Saville, Dunblane GC)

The first holes climb uphill so play long, especially the par 4, 2nd. The 424 yard par 4, 8th is a very good hole that dog-legs left around tall trees. A genuine criticism of Dunblane New is that the eighth, ninth, tenth and twelfth all dog leg in the same direction, the seventeenth being about the only hole that bends right. The course is well bunkered in some areas, none more so than the short eleventh which has five greenside hazards.

The walk from the fourteenth green to the fifteenth tee is through a picturesque stand of tall pines. Cherry blossoms are a feature at Dunblane and one of the prettiest examples is around the seventeenth green. The longest hole at Dunblane is the 561 yard par 5, 18th which runs predominantly downhill. The shot into the green is tight with trees and rough very close by. As this is a wet part of Scotland hope for good weather during your round.

Westwards along the A84 brings us to Callander, the gateway to the Trossachs and just fifteen miles north of Stirling. **Callander** is best described as a wooded parkland course with a number of diverse holes and fun to play. It's weakness is lack of length with seven par 3's and a total length of just 5208 yards.

The sixth, 'Dell', is a lovely par 4 with a plateau green and thick trees along the left side. The seventh is a memorable short par 4 of 300 yards with a blind tee shot. Ten and eleven are back to back par 3's, both approximately 180 yards. The tenth is an attractive tree lined setting whilst at the eleventh you play over a stream to a green with bunkers on both sides.

*Above: The par 3, 15th at Dunblane New in winter
(Photo courtesy Val Saville, Dunblane GC)
Below: Par 3, 15th 'Avenue' with Ben Ledi in the distance
(Photo courtesy Callander GC)*

The fifteenth is aptly named 'Avenue'. It is 136 yards through a small gap in trees on both sides with Ben Ledi framing the background. A large bunker runs across the front of the green so you can't run your ball on to the putting surface. The par 4, 16th has a wide fairway but you need to stay clear of the pond. The only par 5 follows at the seventeenth. The fairway will tend to run your ball to the left and when approaching the green the temptation is to play to the right but this side is protected by a bunker.

Callander is an interesting inland course in a pretty setting. The variety of holes helps negate that it is a rather short.

From Callander the A811 will lead us to the south end of Loch Lomond and then a short distance on the A82 to the golf course and hotel. I had always wanted to play **Loch Lomond** and my plan was to be there just a few days after the Scottish Open was last held there in 2009. We experienced fairly good weather and the course was relatively dry – I believe they had preferred lies at the two previous Scottish Opens. Even so, a few showers in the morning of the day we played

Above: Callander's 18th hole and clubhouse (Photo courtesy Callander GC)
Below: Accurate driving is essential at Loch Lomond

meant that the fairways were playing somewhat longer than the links courses we revisited on the preceeding two days of the 2009 trip.

Men have a choice of three tees. Ignoring the Championship tees, you are either playing 6675 (blue) or 6300 (white) yards. The 16th is a par 5 from these tees but for tournaments this hole becomes a brute of a par 4 at 495 yards. With a burn in front of the green then this makes for a tough second shot.

The first two holes are a good opening and then at the par 5, 3rd you head towards the loch. The 4th green doubles with the 2nd and then before you lies the wonderful par 3, 5th where you hit over wild flowers and grasses nearly four feet high to a green with Loch Lomond as its backdrop. The next few holes are near the loch and run towards the accommodation buildings. At the sixth, the hole bends from left to right and if you drive a little too far left then you will be blocked by several large trees. The par 3, 8th is only 160 yards from the blue tee but is slightly uphill and can pay much longer if you are into even a wee breeze.

The attractive par 3, 5th with Loch Lomond directly behind the green

The middle of the back nine features some treed and moderately hilly areas and the thirteenth which requires precise shot making to avoid the marshy areas. It was here that Tom Weiskopf nearly lost his life after walking into quicksand early one morning during the course construction. The 14th is a short par 4 of 330 yards which dog-legs right so you need to lay up with your tee shot.

The par 3, 17th is a picturesque gem as good as the fifth but this time the loch is along the left. It can be a tough hole at 185 yards with a carry over a wetland with high grasses. One of the best holes from an architectural aspect is undoubtedly the eighteenth, a two shot cape hole which dog-legs

Top: 16th green and burn
Above: The 17th green looks peaceful but this is a tough par 3 of 185 yards with a long carry over wetland and the Loch all along the left side

left around Loch Lomond. When playing into the green you need absolute precision to negotiate the narrow opening.

The greens were excellent and surprisingly fast considering they had just been lightly cored and dusted. The rough was not long but was so thick that your ball literally disappeared if you missed the fairway even only into the first cut. Loch Lomond is a great golfing experience especially if you are lucky enough to catch a still and sunny day in what is, unfortunately, one of the wettest parts of Scotland. The scenery is further enhanced by the numerous Scots Pines, Douglas Firs and ancient oak trees.

For what it is worth, our accommodation in Rossdhu House, a lovely Georgian manor house built in 1773, was excellent but the food was fairly ordinary. Apart from the Weiskopf/Morrish layout the Loch Lomond members also have the Dundonlad Links, a Kyle Phillips design in Ayr on the inland side of Western Gailes.

Nearby, and a little further south, just off the A82 is the town of Arden and **The Carrick** which I have to say, despite some good holes, was a little disappointing.

The front nine is referred to as 'the lowlands' featuring plenty of ponds and lakes. You cross over the river for holes four to eight and it was here that I found many of the fairways to be very wet (in mid summer). The other negative for me was the holes around the tenth and eleventh which, although well designed, were very exposed and seemed to me to be permanently very windy.

There are five sets of tees, the longest being the black (7082 yards) and the white(6729 yards). The opening hole is a good test at 407 yards (white) with bunkers on the left and a wet ditch along the right. The par 3, 2nd plays over the corner of a lake and then you face the rather scary third hole. This is a long par 4 with a small wet area on the left for the drive plus a lake runs all the way on the right finishing greenside.

Top: Rossdhu House, built in 1773
Above: Opening hole at The Carrick

After crossing over the river you are faced with another long par 4, this time bending left around a lake. This fairway was very sodden so I can't imagine what it would be like in the cooler months – pity,

9th hole at The Carrick

The 14th from its very elevated tee

otherwise this would be a good hole. Holes five, seven and eight, two par 5's and a long par 4, are well protected by a number of deep straight faced bunkers. The eighth is the longest of the four par 5's at 588 yards from the white. It is a good looking but demanding hole with trees on the right, pockets of trees and OOB to the left and a total of fourteen bunkers.

From the ninth to the thirteenth you are on exposed high ground but from here on there are some lovely holes alongside Loch Lomond. The par 3, 14th is clearly the signature hole where you play from a dramatic tee high up looking over

15th green as viewed from near the 14th tee

the green 190 yards away. There are five bunkers and then the loch further right. The fifteenth is the last of the par 5's and is aptly named 'Bonnie Banks'. It bends left around the loch and is heavily bunkered near the green.

If you haven't lost a few balls by now then you are doing very well. The par 3, 16th features a pond or lake on the right and gorse then OOB at the left and the rear of a green flanked by five bunkers. Just for good measure the two closing holes are both in excess of 400 yards, the eighteenth being the more difficult with a pond at the left and a marshy area to the right as you get to about 120 yards from the green.

The Carrick is part of the De Vere hotel group. The clubhouse and restaurant was excellent and the staff were all friendly and helpful. From what I could see they were also offering quite good golf and accommodation deals at their on-site Cameron House. Hard to summarise The Carrick as it contained some very good holes but has a problem with some of the wet areas.

Carradale is a very pretty nine hole course on the west coast of the Kintyre Peninsula. I'm not suggesting for one moment that you drive all the way down here just to play Carradale, but if you are visiting Machrihanish and the newer Machrihanish Dunes then this little course is well worth a visit. Despite its relative anonymity it has been in existence since 1906.

You would normally only use the A83 which runs down the west coast of the Kintyre Peninsula. However, one of my recent trips to Machrihanish was followed by a week on the Isle of Arran so we drove along the B842 which runs along the east coast from Campbeltown to the ferry link in the village of Claonaig. About half way along that scenic journey you will find Carradale. Despite its proximity to the sea it is not a links but is closer to a heathland or moorland course.

2nd hole from behind the 4th green

There are wonderful views of wooded hills in one direction and the sea and Kilbrannan Sound in the other. In winter the snow capped peaks on Arran provide the backdrop. The opening par 3 is straight uphill and is followed by a great little par 4 of 329 yards where you play into a valley from an elevated tee to a green near the cliff edge. After a long par 3 along the cliff the fourth heads back uphill toward the 2nd tee. This par 4 is only 287 yards but if you try to drive the green you will more than likely finish in the grassy hummocks half way up the hill. You may be better advised to drive to the bottom of the hill and then it is just a short iron uphill to the plateau green.

The fifth and sixth holes head towards the bay and are followed by Index 1, a par 3 of 240 yards. The final hole is a short par 4 but you will be in plenty of trouble if you duff your drive or pull your shot left toward the water.

What an enjoyable little sporty course this is. There are two sets of tees on this little gem of just 4550 yards. And every now and then you may have to share the fairways with sheep and goats. I can highly recommend the meal at the adjacent Carradale Hotel which provides accommodation as well as meals for the golfers.

Top: 3rd tee and Isle of Arran
Below: Carradale's par 4, 4th hole

Geographically the next port of call would be the Isle of Arran but I intend to cover this in the following chapter. The A78 runs down the west coast of Scotland where the first stop will be the municipal course in Ayr known as **Belleisle**. Next door in Doonfoot Road is another, but somewhat shorter course, **Seafield**, which has something of a links feel on many holes.

Belleisle is a James Braid creation of 1927. Many regard it as one of the premier inland courses in Scotland but I am not quite that impressed. It is certainly a very good municipal course but I don't think there are many stand out holes in this parkland layout of 6446 yards. It is well treed and there are some good views across to Arran. Seven of the nine par 4's exceed 400 yards, none better than the sixth which sweeps down to a smallish green with bunkers either side.

Rather uniquely, Belleisle begins and finishes with a par 5. After the par 3, 17th, where you play across water, the eighteenth is a good par 5 of 532 yards which dog-legs right. The fairways are reasonably expansive but they are also well bunkered. Belleisle is a popular public course so you might be in for a slow round.

The A78 becomes the coastal A77 heading well south to the ferry terminal town of Stranraer. The course at **Stranraer** was James Braid's last design and opened as recently as 1959. You will find it on the A718, higher up about three miles from the town and overlooking Loch Ryan.

Most of the course is several hundred feet above sea level but the real stand out is the par 4, 5th which runs right along the beach. If the water on the right causes you to hook left then you will probably finish in thick gorse. A burn is in play on a number of holes such as the second where it runs across, the third where it is all down the right and the twelfth which has the burn in front of the green.

After the brilliant 5th hole there is a par 3 of 160 yards. The tee is played from near the sea to a green with six bunkers. Trees line both sides of this pretty hole. The 11th tee is high up on the course and provides wonderful views to Ailsa Craig and Arran.

Lovely trees are a feature at Ayr Belleisle (Photo courtesy Paul Walker Images)

The 14th is the only par 5 (513 yards) and is just as good a hole as the fifth. It dog-legs left along the waters edge and has three strategic bunkers – one short and two beside the green. It seems sad to think that the eighteenth was Braid's last - a par 4 of only 343 yards but very well bunkered in the latter half of the hole.

It had been some time since I was last at Stranraer so I thought I should contact the Secretary. Perhaps they don't want visitors as they did not reply to any of my emails or the letter I subsequently sent in desperation.

Portpatrick lies right on the coast on the A77 about seven miles beyond Stranraer. The **Portpatrick Dunskey Golf Club** consists of the eighteen hole Dunskey Course and a shorter nine hole course known as the Dinvin. The Dunskey is cliff top and the heavier soil precludes it from being of the links variety.

It measures just under 6000 yards but there are some very good holes here. The second hole which heads towards the sea and the little village of Portpatrick pretty much sets the scene. The par 5, 3rd is rated Index 1 and measures a healthy 544 yards. The drive is demanding and the second shot requires a blind lay up. There is plenty of gorse waiting for wayward shots. At the par 3, 4th you play over a gully and need to take an extra club as it tends to play longer than 160 yards. The par 3, 7th 'Gorsebank' is an excellent short hole with a narrow green and plenty of trouble if you miss. It plays uphill but being through the back of the green is not the place to be.

The tenth is an excellent par 4 that heads towards the sea. It is not long but OOB is very much in play along the left. Each of the par 3's are good holes and the eleventh is no exception with its very undulating green.

Without doubt, the thirteenth, 'Sandeel', is one of the most spectacular short par 4's you will ever play. At 293 yards and downhill it is reachable from the tee. Cliffs run along the left with OOB along the Irish Sea. A new bunker has been added short and right of the green which slopes toward the cliffs. Behind the green is a magnificent backdrop of hills, rocky cliffs and an inlet where the sea has eaten into the eroded landscape. If the wind is howling in from the left, I dare you to start your tee shot towards the sea and watch your ball (hopefully) land back on the rather wide fairway.

Sandeel, the spectacular 13th hole at Portpatrick

On my first visit here I was mesmerized by this hole. I spent about an hour taking photographs and watching to see how the locals played it. One of my photos of Sandeel became the cover photo of my second book Fairways in Heaven, Bunkers from Hell which was published in Australia back in 1999.

Portpatrick finishes with a good par 5 of 535 yards. Be careful to avoid the three bunkers on the right hand side of the green. The fairways and greens were excellent as was the ambience in the clubhouse. This is a lovely location for some relaxing holiday golf. Portpatrick is primarily a fishing village and the off-season population is under 1000. It can be a bit tricky trying to find the golf club. Just before you reach the village, turn into Heligh Road which will then lead you to Golf Club Road. You will also pass the highly regarded Fernhill Hotel which is just a short walk from the clubhouse.

This completes the Scottish journey except for a visit to the delightful Isle of Arran which is the subject of the next chapter.

There are many superb views from the coastal road that circumnavigates Arran

ISLE OF ARRAN

Arran lies between the Firth of Clyde and Kilbrannan Sound facing the Kintyre Peninsula. This magical little island is the seventh largest in Scotland and measures nineteen miles in length and is just ten miles wide. Despite its small size it has a great variety of scenery with the north being the more hilly. Climate and weather can vary dramatically with the east side generally being protected from the elements.

My wife and I spent a delightful week there during summer. If it rained on one part of Arran you could usually drive for ten minutes and find sunshine on the other side. Getting to Arran from just north of Ayr is very easy as the excellent car ferry service from Ardrossan to Brodick takes less than an hour. If you are coming from the Kintyre Peninsula, as we were, then it is only a thirty minute journey by ferry from Claonaig to Lochranza on the north of the island.

There are plenty of good B & B's and hotels to choose from and most are well located near little villages along the coastline. We opted for a lovely B & B just walking distance to the shops and golf course at Brodick. The population here is a little over 5000 and tourism is the main industry. Apart from golf there is wonderful scenery everywhere such as Brodick Castle, the standing stones at Machrie Moor and the often snow clad Goatfell are just some of the attractions.

Brodick's par 4, 1st hole with Goatfell in the distance

Believe it or not, this tiny island has seven golf courses. I would not bother about the nine holers at Lochranza, Corrie or Machrie Bay but the rest are all worth a visit. Corrie and Machrie Bay each have a few good holes but they are both very short courses. Corrie is hilly and more inland whilst Machrie Bay's best are along the waters edge. You can pretty much see all of the course from the coastal road and if you are in the area then it is worth visiting the tea rooms nearby.

Brodick is an easy walking eighteen holes and is a mixture of wooded parkland and some holes which have more of a heathland links feel. The opening hole is a good straight par 4 of 401 yards that plays over a burn in front of the tee and is dominated by the view of Goatfell in the distance. A short par 4 and then a short par 3 follow before you enter a quaint wooded part of the course. The par 3, 4th requires a well struck tee shot over the River Rosa.

The fifth is rated Index 1 and is the only par 5 at Brodick. The second shot is played through a narrow gap between two large fir trees. There is a wet area on the right that may catch your second strike and then another wet area on the left as you approach the green. The par 4, 6th is a lovely shaped hole amongst the trees where you play to a kidney shaped green. The green at the short seventh is almost blocked by trees —you need to be dead straight or perhaps hit a slight fade. At the 167 yard par 3, 8th the best approach is a slight draw to the small elevated green with OOB on the right and trees to the left. The Index rating of 3 gives some idea as to the potential danger here. The ninth is a good par 4 but avoid the thickly grassed wet area on the left.

The first few holes of the back nine are gorse-lined fairways on low lying land right beside the sea. From the twelfth to the fifteenth is a succession of short holes each of which are rather different. One of the best is the 15th which is only 121 yards. The tee shot is across the river to a green scarily close to the sea. With a following wind this green is very difficult to hold. Anything short or left is in the water. Looking back from the green, Brodick Castle rises from above the trees on its hillside advantage point overlooking Brodick Bay.

The 18th is an extremely difficult par 3 of 222 yards. A wide burn must be carried and then there is a steep slope up to

Par 3, 4th hole plays across the River Rosa

the green. Anything slightly to the right will leave your next shot blocked by trees. From the back (white) tees Brodick has eight par 3's – each with a different feel. It is harder if you play off the yellow tees as then the second, twelfth, sixteenth and seventeenth holes change from short par 4's to very long par 3's. Brodick is lots of fun and well worth playing but given its lack of length then you would only want to play from the back tees. The greens are small but are good and the people in the clubhouse are very friendly.

A few miles south of Brodick is the very challenging **Lamlash**. Until the end of the First World War Lamlash Bay was used as a base by Britain's Atlantic Fleet. The present course dates back to the late 1890's when it was laid out by Willie Auchterlonie. There are some exciting holes at Lamlash, but be warned, this is a very hilly course, particularly for the first eleven holes, so you need to be reasonably fit if you are going to enjoy the experience.

Top: *When the tide is in, the 15th green is right beside the water at Brodick*
Below: *Index 1, 'Goatfell', the 3rd hole with its severely sloping fairway at Lamlash*

The opening hole is a tough start as you play up a very steep hill. The tee shot on this par 4 needs to avoid the burn in front of the tee and then along the left of the fairway. The third is a par 4 of 387 yards but it plays much longer. Apart from the sloping fairway you must also contend with a burn at the bottom of the gully about forty yards short of the green. Anywhere left at the par 3, 5th or par 4, 6th and your ball will run into a wet area with thick bracken.

Holes seven, eight, ten, eleven and fifteen are rather difficult long par 3's from the yellow tees but are somewhat easier

The first hole at Lamlash is a steep introduction

par 4's being only about fifty yards longer from the white tees. After a steep climb at the tenth and eleventh the remaining holes are either fairly flat or play downhill. From the tenth green are some of the best views to nearby Holy Island.

I would not recommend you play off the yellow (visitors) tees if you can avoid it, otherwise holes ten to seventeen are all par 3's all of which are very long except for

Above: Holy Island from the 10th tee
Below: The short 16th 'Wee Dunt'

the 16th. The 16th 'Wee Dunt' is the only really short hole at just 98 yards but it can be difficult to know just how hard to hit your tee shot which is down-hill to a green with thick bracken at the front and a wet grassy gully at the back.

It's not over till it's over and the eighteenth can ruin a good card. The second shot on this par 4 is over a gully and through a very narrow gap in the trees to an elevated green.

Parts of Lamlash were a bit damp so I guess it could get rather soggy here in winter. A degree of difficulty is added by having small greens but Lamlash does suffer from having a very limited amount of space in which to squeeze in eighteen holes.

Four miles further south is the village of Whiting Bay. On higher ground above the village is **Whiting Bay** Golf Club, a pretty parkland course with breathtaking views from most holes. Although this is predominantly parkland there are a number of holes with gorse and heather giving it something of a heathland feel. It may be very short at just 4063 yards but five of the nine par 3's are over 200 yards in length.

The first four holes climb upwards to more of a plateau. The fourth is the shortest hole at 81 yards but can still prove to be difficult as it plays up a steep hill to a very small raised green.

The next six holes play mainly across the hillside where gorse and heather is an added hazard. The par 4, 8th is rated the hardest and the short par 4, 10th requires a blind drive uphill. At the short eleventh you are at the highest part of the course so enjoy the magnificent views of Holy Island and the

Top: The short 4th at Whiting Bay from behind the green
Middle: 8th hole from in front of the tee. The zig-zag path in the distance behind the green runs up to the 'Giants Graves', a 5000 year old Neolithic tomb on the shoulder of the hill.
Above: 13th from behind and Holy island in the distance
(Photos courtesy Whiting Bay GC)

nearby countryside. This hole can be very tricky with OOB to the left, deep rough on the right and a green that is raised.

The twelfth is another blind drive – always a scary proposition when you don't know the course. It is a short par 4 over a heather clad hill but don't go through the back of the green. At the fourteenth you play across the hill directly in line with Holy Island. Sixteen and seventeen are uphill again before you descend down the last hole which slopes to the right where there is OOB. The green is frighteningly close to the clubhouse.

Whiting Bay is worth playing just for the views alone. If it is a warm sunny day then there is no better spot for a drink and reminisce than the patio beside the clubhouse.

Continuing on the coastal road it is now to the south western side of Arran to the brilliant and quirky **Shiskine** located near the village of Blackwaterfoot and overlooking Drumadoon Bay. As the crow flies this is not too far from Campbeltown on the west coast of the Mull of Kintyre.

Above: The 18th green is right beside the clubhouse. Above the clubhouse roof line, is the PS Waverley – the last ocean going paddle steamer in the world (Photo courtesy Whiting Bay GC)
Below: Looking towards the 3rd hole at Shiskine

I have explained earlier in the book that I have included Shiskine even though it is clearly a links. I have done this for two reasons. Firstly, because it is only twelve holes it was not in either of my books featuring all the eighteen hole links in the UK and Ireland and, secondly, you could not write about golf on Arran and omit Shiskine.

In the mid 1890's Arran had not escaped the boom in golf course development in Scotland. (I have avoided using the word 'construction' because in many cases very little soil was moved in building these natural courses). Willie Fernie designed nine holes and then a little later another nine. During the First World War some of the holes fell into neglect and Shiskine became twelve holes.

Just like other similar links with many blind shots(for example, The Machrie at Islay) you must experience Shiskine at least twice to get some understanding of how to play the holes.

Unless you hit a long drive you commence with semi blind shots to the greens on each of the first two par 4 holes. You are then confronted with the incredibly alluring par 3 'Crows Nest'. Forget the distance of 128 yards. You must play up a very steep hill to a green high up that is protected at the front by a ridge of rocks and gorse about five feet high. Anything even a fraction short will probably ricochet into the bushes. You cannot see the pin position from the tee but a separate red flag is raised by players leaving the green so that you know when it is safe to hit.

From this area on the side of the hill you then play a par 3 of 146 yards with the green way below and the sea beyond. There are fabulous views from here to all parts of the course. The fifth is aptly named 'Point'. It is a long par 3 of 243 yards that plays along the coast-line to another green close to the water at the far corner of the layout.

The 3rd green 'Crows Nest'. The red flag tells when it is safe to hit from the tee.

4th green at Shiskine

The par 4, 6th is a wonderful hole with the green hidden in a dell with thick bracken to the left and the rear where there is also a wet area. 'Himalayas' tells you that the next hole will be a blind par 3, in this case over a bracken covered hill. The eighth, like the sixth, is a short par 4 that is a birdie chance if you get a good drive away.

The 506 yard ninth is the only par 5. The second shot must be played over a gully and then a burn which is one of the two that run right across the links. If there is a let down then it is the final three holes that are all par 3's. The eleventh is quite a challenge at 209 yards to a sloping green in a hollow but the final hole was an anti-climactic 128 yards.

They have a weird system for visitors that I did not like. Both men and women play from the yellow markers that are more or less the same distance as the lady member's red tees. Notwithstanding the above, this is a fine little links that is great fun to play but with most of the tees and greens so close together you don't want to pick a day with a hacker spraying balls from one fairway to another.

A week of good weather on Arran will pass very quickly as you explore the golfing and scenic delights.

Top: Short par 4, 6th at sunset. Above: Par 3, 11th – 'The Hollows' (Photos courtesy Hamish Bannatyne)

NORTHERN ENGLAND

Generally speaking, it is the heathland that appeals to me most when it comes to playing the inland or non-links courses and England has some fantastic examples, particularly in and around Surrey. Before embarking on a heathland trail heading down to London there are several courses in the north that definitely warrant a visit.

You could not start at a more idyllic setting than **Windermere** Golf Club in the magical Lake District in England's north west. If you are continuing on from a Scottish adventure and you are coming from Portpatrick then you can either choose the A75, M6, A6 and link up with the A591 at Kendall or at Penrith you take the more scenic A592.

When I first visited I was not even aware there was a golf course in the vicinity as it is hidden away near the B5284 one mile east of Bowness. Each time I have played here they have been very welcoming. On the first occasion, back in 1998, my wife and I were soaked after our round and happened to be standing outside the Secretary's office when he emerged. He took one look at us and offered us a free round if we cared to return on a better day. Of course we gladly accepted.

More recently we were staying at Lakeside and, being a saturday in summer, I assumed we would not be able to play so I decided to settle for just getting some new photographs. I clearly remember driving into the car park at about 11.30 am on a sunny day and there were only four cars there. I always have the clubs in the boot so I was delighted to find that golf would not be a problem but best to hit off before midday.

They call Windermere the 'miniature Gleneagles' which I think is very appropriate. The club has a long history with its first nine holes completed in 1891 and the second nine a year later under the direction of George Lowe, the professional at Lytham & St Annes.

The club's official history records an unusual complaint in early 1939 via the Suggestions Book: "In a recent Four Ball Match, one of the players lost the 16th hole owing to the sudden arrival, at a menacing gallop, of a dog, thought

Windermere – 1st tee, Pro shop and clubhouse

to belong to the Hon. Sec. and the same player lost the 18th hole, and the match, because the Steward's 'Tiny Tot' molested him by annexing his ball after his drive and hiding it under the Teddy Bear in her perambulator. Suggested that the Hon. Sec.'s livestock and the Steward's progeny be kept under proper control." I very much doubt that such a complaint today would be put so eloquently!

The opening hole is a short par 4 that heads uphill through the rocky outcrops. The second is the longest of the par 3's at 231 yards. Accuracy is essential as OOB awaits you on the left and thick rough runs along the right. A relatively easy short par 4 is then followed by the more difficult 4th where you need to drive to the right to enable your blind second strike to hopefully hold the green which slopes from the left.

The fifth bends to the left and also needs an accurate drive. Anything hooked may finish in a pond and a long drive leaked to the right will find heather. The next two holes can cause problems with rocks on the right and bracken to the left to be avoided with the tee shot. A pond on the left is in play for your approach at the sixth and there are rocks near the green at the dog-leg seventh.

5th hole from behind

Picture postcard view of neighbouring farmland beside the 8th tee at Windermere

Par 3, 8th

The par 3, 8th is 148 yards over a bracken-clad hollow to a plateau green that seems to be a very small target with no bail out area. The scenery to the left of the tee is a post card view of the Lake District. Both the ninth and tenth play from elevated tees followed by the reverse at the eleventh. The par 4, 12th is rather more difficult as it has a burn crossing the fairway about 220 yards from the tee and the hole then turns left to a narrow green. The thirteenth green is in a pretty setting with a stone wall at the back.

The short fourteenth will be unforgiving if you miss the green on either side but particularly the right. Another par 3 follows at the 15th but this is somewhat longer at 190 yards. This is a lovely looking hole that plays downhill. The burn that cuts across and then runs along the right is only in play for a poor shot.

The only par 5 at Windermere is the 464 yard 16th. The fairway is narrow and slopes left where there are large trees, OOB and then the road. The par 4, 17th is rated the second hardest. First, your drive must clear

The 17th is justifiably rated index 2

The tranquil view from our room at Lakeside Hotel

The 9th at Windermere is one of many good short par 4's

the rocky outcrops, and then the ground falls away sharply to the left. If you are too far right, speaking from experience, you will encounter grassy mounds, heather and trees. To add to the challenge, the hole dog-legs right to a two-tiered green. The final hole is a tough par 3 of 204 yards up a steep hill with a little hillock guarding the green.

Windermere is somewhat hilly but how could you not enjoy the atmosphere here. The clubhouse looks down the eighteenth fairway and features large garden beds with bright yellows, oranges and reds alongside the white brickwork.

There is plenty of accommodation especially nearby at Ambleside or you might consider the lovely hotel overlooking the water at Lakeside. On a sunny day a boat cruise is a must and you can also visit Beatrix Potter's house at Hawkeshead, about five miles from Windermere. A few miles further down the A591 you will find Sizergh Castle and Leven Hall which has one of the best topiary displays in Britain.

In the northern parts of England you have the opportunity to play a number of layouts designed by Dr Alister MacKenzie. On pretty much the same latitude as Windermere and eleven miles inland from Scarborough on the east coast is the MacKenzie designed **Ganton**. This is a top class course but is not included in this book as I have classified it as having the unique distinction of being an 'inland links'. For this reason it features in my books on links courses where I have set out in more detail as to why it is a links.

Having planned to start my 'heathland trail' trip around Leeds before gradually heading down to London, I kept a few days clear so as to take advantage of any recommendations to play courses that were less well known to me in my far away Melbourne, Australia. One such suggestion was that I should play Pannal, located a few miles south of Harrogate. From the Lake District we travelled there via the A65, A59 and then a short distance along the A61.

Pannal was originally laid out in 1906 by Alex Herd on land leased from Lord Harewood. At this time it was common practice for new clubs to publicise the opening of their course with a 'celebrity match' with well known professionals. And so it was at Pannal where two of the greats, James Braid and Harry Vardon played a match at the official opening of the full course in 1908.

My wife and I thoroughly enjoyed our round at Pannal. Whilst it is more wooded parkland than heathland, they are

Pannal's par 3, 3rd hole

currently in the process of removing much of the gorse and restoring the heath. In places it is rather hilly but this helps provide for some very picturesque views, especially from around the middle of the back nine. The conditioning of the fairways and greens was excellent.

The round commences with two formidable par 4's over 400 yards. The second hole, although shorter, is probably slightly the more difficult due to the dog-leg left and OOB. The green at the par 3, 3rd features three bunkers at the left and a larger one short right.

Index 1 at Pannal is the long par 4, 6th which bends right to left over a hill. If you miss the green there is a nasty hollow to the left and OOB at the rear. Pannal has many pretty settings and none better than the eighth green nestled among the pine trees. The tenth is the shortest of the par 3's measuring just 142 yards. However, your tee shot is partly blocked by trees on both sides.

Top right: Watch the trees at the 10th
Right: Looking to the 6th green from the 17th green
Below: 17th green and Crimple Viaduct

Eleven, twelve and thirteen comprise two short par 5's and a long par 4 (12th). The twelfth is not just long at 459 yards but there is the added hazard by way of a large oak that partly blocks the drive. One of the very memorable holes is the par 3, 17th with its fabulous views across the countryside to the famous Crimple Viaduct – the subject of many paintings. The length is testing at 190 yards and the green is set into the side of the hill with everything sloping to the right. Left is OOB and there are three deep bunkers, two on the right.

The eighteenth tee is high up and invites you to give your utmost as you hit down a steep hill to the green. From the tee you are looking

Above: The par 4, 18th invites a big drive
Below: Pannal's lovely clubhouse and practice putting green

straight towards Crimple Valley. Your main danger here is OOB which runs all the way down the left of the fairway. It may have been 'beginners luck', but I found the back nine holes to be a little easier than the first nine.

The clubhouse possesses a lovely painting of Bobby Locke who was stationed nearby with the RAF during the Second World War. The club's history relates that "older members remember seeing him, after he had played at Pannal, sitting at the bar playing his ukulele; the 17th hole was said to be his favourite."

On a sunny day the patio outside the bar is a great place to relax and watch the golf. We found the meals here to be very good and the Secretary, Neil Douglas, could not have been more helpful. I am confident you will enjoy your day at Pannal and, after all, golf is meant to be fun.

Heading south to Leeds there are two courses that are clearly the best in this area, namely Alwoodley and Moortown. In the moorland countryside just to the north of the city you might also consider **Sand Moor** and **Moor Allerton** but from my quick observation they did not look to be in the same class.

My round at **Alwoodley** was all the more interesting as I was accompanied by well known member, Nick Leefe, a past Captain of the club and Secretary of the Alister MacKenzie Society. Having teamed up with Harry Colt, this was MacKenzie's first involvement in an eighteen hole design around 1907.

Alwoodley is more than a solid test of your golf – it just never lets up. Wayward driving will be penalized in every instance either by gorse or heather and thick rough. From a photographic perspective it was interesting that in early and mid July the heather was not quite in flower but by the end of the month as we had progressed a little further south the pink and purple flowers were unfolding in spectacular fashion.

Avoid the heather at the 5th at Alwoodley

The stroke index ratings here are very old and are based on match play so can be a little misleading. The opening hole is a good par 4 of about 400 yards to get the field away. The second may be a short par 4 but there are trees and heather on both sides of this lovely hole where four bunkers await you at the green. The third and fourth are each par 5's but the fourth is decidedly more difficult if played off the yellow tees where it is reduced to a par 4.

Above: Par 3, 11th
Below: Looking across the 16th and 4th greens

The 5th is a very pretty par 4 with a fairway that slopes to the right where the heather is at its thickest. The 6th is a longer version of the previous hole and is very well bunkered for the second shot. The shortest of the par 3's is the 7th (143 yards) which has a fairly narrow green and five bunkers. Index 1 is the par 5, 8th that sweeps left. If you cut too much off the corner you may find trees or OOB. The three level green adds a bit more to the degree of difficulty.

The tenth is another long hole which dog-legs left and is followed by the

Top: The 17th green is hidden when you are playing your second shot at this par 4
Above: The 18th at Alwoodley and the distinctive clubhouse

very scenic 167 yard par 3, 11th where there is a burn in front of the tee and then a green with four bunkers and a steep slope if you miss to the left. The twelfth is not the place for a wayward tee shot as thick gorse runs for about 180 yards. The thirteenth needs to be played very precisely so as to avoid two cross bunkers at about 180 yards, two more bunkers further on to the left, heather and gorse at the right and another four bunkers near the green.

The longest par 3 is the 14th and at 206 yards the plateau green is a difficult target. I remember the 16th well having fallen foul of the thick rough. A pond lies in front of the tee of this tricky two shotter. Two bunkers may catch any drive too far left but thick rough and heather runs along the right.

The penultimate hole is a rather unusual long par 4. You need to avoid OOB at the left and then the hole turns sharply to the right where you play blind to a green thirty feet below the level of the fairway. If you cut off too much of the corner then you will encounter a rather large bunker on the side of the slope above the green.

Many of the holes on the back nine are all the more difficult as they play into the prevailing wind. This makes the 446 yard 18th a very demanding par 4. It is an excellent finishing hole that is visually dominated by the unusual looking clubhouse. You will have played very well if you beat your handicap at Alwoodley.

Nearby **Moortown** is a woodland and moorland course with plenty of variety amongst its eighteen holes which stretch to nearly 7000 yards from the championship tees. Dr. Alister MacKenzie not only designed Moortown but he was the inaugural Chairman in 1909 and Club Captain in 1913. In 1929 the first Ryder Cup to be played on English soil was held here. In cold and raw weather an estimated 20,000 watched over the two days as George Duncan's team were victorious 7-5 over the United states team captained by Walter Hagen.

Don't be short at the par 3, 4th at Moortown

From the white tees Moortown is 6747 yards and even from the yellow it is long enough at 6452 yards. A short par 5 at the opening is followed by a very testing par 4 of 440 yards (white tees). Your long second shot needs to miss the three greenside bunkers. The third is of similar length and is lined with trees on both sides as it narrows towards the green. The bunkers are well short of the green at the par 3, 4th so this plays a little longer than you expect. Anything well short will be in long grass.

10th green as seen from side on at the 7th green

Whilst the fifth is a shorter par 4, it dog-legs sharply left and is bunkered along the right.

The 6th (446 yards) is one of seven par 4's that are each well over 400 yards from the white tees. Six of them are still over 400 yards even from the yellow. From the seventh green there are lovely side on views through the trees to the tenth green.

One of MacKenzie's great holes is the 172 yards par 3, 10th 'Gibraltar'. The green slopes to the left where there is a large bunker just short of the putting surface. The lie of the land makes you want to head for the right hand side of the green but if you are a wee too far right then three bunkers and some nasty rough awaits you.

Holes eleven through to thirteen are very heathland in feel and you will be doing well if you haven't played at least one shot from the heather, particularly at twelve and thirteen. The fourteenth and fifteenth are slightly shorter par 4's but they are strategically bunkered and anything left will be in the thick line of trees. The par 4, 16th has a burn running diagonally across the fairway and then again in front of the tee at the par 3, 17th. Despite being rated the easiest at Moortown, the 17th plays 155 yards steeply uphill with a bunker short and left then three more beside the sloping green.

Moortown's famous 10th, 'Gibraltar'

Mootown's eighteenth is a terrific finish. The hole plays uphill and bends right to a green that is scarily close to the clubhouse windows. Trees run along the left and bunkers protect the right hand side of the fairway.

I love the serendipitous way you make friends in golf. Some years ago my good friend from Glasgow, Duncan Martin, was at the Ryder Cup in the USA where he struck up a conversation with Bob Seaton who was at the time the Captain at Moortown. Bob mentioned that he was later going to Australia to play in a MacKenzie event at Royal Melbourne and with that Duncan said he could arrange a game at Commonwealth with myself. Bob and I had a wonderful day at Commonwealth (my home club) and, to cut a long story short, I initiated steps that led to reciprocity between Moortown and Commonwealth. On the occasion of my first visit to Moortown I presented them with a photograph of the 11th hole at Commonwealth which now hangs in their dining room.

My wife and I revisited Moortown a second time on our 2011 journey and once again we were made exceedingly welcome by Bob Seaton and David Sheret who had been Captain in 2007. On both trips our drive into Leeds in mid summer was accompanied by lashing rain but fortunately the weather improved marginally for our golf.

Moortown has recently restored a number of the original MacKenzie bunkers. My only criticism is that I personally don't like white sand. I believe that the best bunkers are those that blend more into the landscape which is really a feature of MacKenzie's design at courses such as Royal Melbourne.

The tree lined par 4, 15th (Photo courtesy Bob Seaton)

FROM LEEDS TO LONDON

One of my favourite links is undoubtedly Formby near Southport, Liverpool. It has a great ambience and has the unique situation of the Formby Ladies course which is inside the Championship course. On reflection, the beauty of Formby is that the tree lined fairways protect you from the wind that can be merciless at a seaside links but the fairways still run hard and bouncy in summer like a true links. Furthermore, most of the fairways are bordered by heather rather than gorse.

For me, this sums up the attributes of heathland layouts that abound particularly around Surrey. In planning a specific trip that would be a heathland adventure it pretty much meant a journey from Leeds to London in which I plotted a trail that would encompass some thirty courses.

Until around the early 1890's virtually all the inland courses were in downland or parkland settings and, in many cases, proved to be very heavy under foot for much of the year. Referring to the new phenomenon of courses such as Sunningdale, Woking and Worplesdon, Bernard Darwin commented in 1910: 'Meanwhile, however, a new star, the star of heather and sand, has arisen out of the darkness… The idea of hacking and digging and building a course out of land on which two blades of grass do not originally grow together is a comparatively modern one. The elder 'architects' took a piece of country that was more or less ready to their hand, rolled it and mowed it, cut some trenches and built some ramparts, and there was the course. They did not as a rule think of taking a primaeval pine forest or a waste of heather and forcibly turning it into a course; if they had thought of it, moreover, they would not have had the money to carry it out. Now the glorious golfing properties of this country of sand and heather and fir trees have been discovered; its owners too have discovered that they possessed all unknowingly a gold mine from which can be extracted so many hundreds of pounds an acre, and the work of building courses out of the heather and building houses all round it goes gaily on.'[1].

In all of my many previous trips, usually during May to July, it had only been at Royal County Down and Walton Heath in early August where I had seen the heather flowering. My most recent journey was a forty two day trip from mid July to early September specifically so as to hope for good photographs of the heather. I must admit to feeling something of a let down after playing the first ten courses and seeing only patches of flowering heather at Woodhall Spa but nothing at the others.

Most of the courses on my list that were closer to London needed a fair amount of advance booking so it wasn't

Irene 'enjoying' the heather at The Berkshire

[1] *The Golf Courses of the British Isles, Bernard Darwin (first published 1910)*

always possible to play each venue in the exact geographic order that one would desire. I'm not sure if it was because we were further south or because another few weeks had elapsed but by the time we played our first game down south, at The Berkshire, the heather was flowering in breathtaking proportions. I was advised by the locals that 2011 was one of the best years ever for the heather – a combination of a cool Winter followed by an unusually dry Spring.

On the way south from Leeds we played Cavendish at the behest of Nick Leefe, followed by Lindrick and Notts. I would dearly love to visit Notts again when the heather is in flower. It was rather dry when we were in Central England but by the time we were near London it was unusual weather with heavy rain often in the mornings followed by better afternoon conditions.

After Notts we ventured to Sherwood Forest Golf Club, Woodhall Spa, Beau Desert, Little Aston, Woburn, Ashridge and finally Berkhamsted.

If you are going to Woodhall Spa then anyone with a sense of history has to make some time to visit the Petwood Hotel here. It is a beautiful old Tudor style building in lovely grounds and was the base for the Dambusters Squadron. For any younger readers who don't know their story – they flew Lancaster Bombers during the Second World War and, like so many British air crew, suffered a very high mortality rate.

The Petwood Hotel, Woodhall Spa – home of the Dambusters Squadron

Apart from their effort in destroying two of the dams in the Ruhr Valley in Germany they also sank the German battleship Turpitz in just twelve minutes with their huge 'tall boy' bombs. To destroy the dams they had to develop a bouncing bomb that would skip and then sink at the dam's edge and to do this their dangerous sortie required them to fly at just sixty feet. There is much memorabilia inside the hotel including a photograph I found very moving. It is of the squadron, led by Group Captain Cheshire, taken in 1942 with the airman seated or in some cases standing on the wings of a Lancaster bomber. Only a small number survived, some of whom signed the photograph. By far the best portrayal of the Dambusters story is the 1955 movie starring Michael Redgrave and Richard Todd.

I always keep a few days free of organized golf so that we can act upon recommendations to play courses that I may not have considered. Several of my contacts in the UK suggested we should play Beau Desert in Staffordshire. As our only spare day whilst we were in that location was a Saturday I was resigned to just walking the course and taking a few photographs. It was a beautiful sunny day and, not surprisingly, the earliest we could get a game was after 4.00 pm.

I have been in Britain enough times to know that when the sun shines then you take your photos because anything could happen an hour or two later. Having ventured to the first tee with my camera I struck up a conversation with two members – I dearly wish I could remember their full names, but it was Phil and

Practice putting green at Little Aston

Terry (a past Captain). On hearing of our plight they very kindly insisted we join them for their 12.30 tee time which was in just five minutes. Their kindness will be rewarded in part by my positive review of Beau Desert in the next chapter.

Just south of Beau Desert is Little Aston where we were booked to play on the Sunday. The entrance is down a wooded lane that runs by some very expensive looking homes. The small, gated, car park was almost empty which I thought a little odd given it was a Sunday and the weather was perfect for golf. The clubhouse appeared to be very nice inside but what a strange atmosphere. The girl in what purported to be the 'pro shop' really didn't know a golf club from a banjo. Inside, the clubhouse was pretty much in total darkness, the steward did not respond to the bell on the counter and we could not even get a sandwich there. I guess that is the result of having only about 160 members.

After our pleasant round I noticed a young boy having some putting lessons from his father on what is just about the prettiest practice putting green I have ever seen. The father was the son of John Beharell who had been responsible for much of the putting green and the magnificent garden beds. John Beharell won the British Amateur at Troon in 1956 and in 1998 he was Captain of the R & A. Sadly, he died in December 2010.

Hankley Common has acres of heather on nearly every hole

Even though we couldn't get any food on the Sunday, you could not wish for a better setting to relax with a drink than the patio in front of the lounge looking over the putting green and gardens.

Woburn is a magnificent complex with three really top courses and a first class clubhouse. Our arrival however was soon tinged with sadness as we learnt that the day before Alex Hay had died. Alex had been the professional at Woburn and was one of my very favourite tournament golf commentators.

Another interesting experience in central England was at Ashridge where Henry Cotton was the professional for many years. In the year of our visit the Captain at Ashridge was none other than my friend Bill McCreadie who I dealt with at Aurum Press in London. Aurum published my two previous books on links courses.

Bill and I always have an enjoyable bit of match play which is all the more fun when the handicaps are similar. I had one of those embarrassing days that can happen when you play a course you don't know. Each time we got to a tricky green Bill would be telling me how difficult it could be only for me to sink a curling thirty foot putt. But Bill

Above: Atlantic Wall plaque
Below: Above: The remains of the Atlantic Wall

then employed his secret weapon. Only in England and Scotland do you see golfers with dogs tied to their trolleys whilst they are on the course. In Bill's case the dog was not tied up and knew to always run to the green and pick up my ball in its mouth if I was close to the flag!

We took a chance and booked the same B & B for nearly two weeks for part of our stay in the Surrey area. It was somewhat 'off the beaten track' close to a little village called Tilford near the town of Farnham. Apart from the fact that our hosts John and Jane Johns were marvellous, we were only about a mile from Hankley Common Golf Club. If you want to see heather then this is the place. Much of the hillsides here have acres of heather and the golf club is actually exporting some of its own heather to other clubs.

A bridle path runs past the long par 3, 11th at Hankley Common. If you venture about 50 yards off the fairway you will come across the Atlantic Wall. During the lead up to the D Day invasion the Canadian troops practised their artillery here. The wall that they fired at was made of special reinforced concrete so as to replicate the defences built by the Germans in northern France. If you walk another hundred yards through the woods you will see rolling hills of heather and the Nissen huts which had housed the Canadians.

When you are staying in the one place for a while and it is a fair drive to the nearest town then you start thinking about evening meals. If you play Hankley Common or you are staying in the area then you just have to eat at the Duke of Cambridge Hotel which is right beside the entrance to the car park at Hankley Common. Whilst we were there in August 2011 they picked up the prestigious award for best pub meals in south east England – not a bad effort if you consider how many little village pubs there must be in the south east. Your host, Paul, is a keen golfer. I'm sure he will make you even more welcome if you tell him that you had been recommended to his pub by David and Irene from Australia.

I recall saying in *Journey through the Links* that my non-golfing friends seem to think that all links courses are the same. They might think along the same lines after you tell them that you are going to England to play thirty heathland courses. What wonderful variety we found at each of them where I can vividly remember so many of the holes.

Courses such as West Hill, Woking, Worplesdon, Swinley Forest, The Berkshire, St George's Hill, Sunningdale and New Zealand are not just heathland but they are also beautifully treed, usually with Scots Pines and the like.

Liphook and The Addington have their share of slightly quirky holes and then there is the very hilly Royal Ashdown Forest with views across the county. At some courses you will play across bridle tracks and I recall that at West Sussex and Liphook the riders clearly felt that the golf course was their domain and the golfers would just have to be patient whilst they ambled across the fairway. To quote the great Bernard Darwin, there is no doubt that all these courses represent "an endless variety of battle fields."

West Hill's beautiful tree lined 8th hole

CENTRAL ENGLAND

Several of my friends from Royal Melbourne had urged me to play the rural, out of the way, 1925 MacKenzie design called **Cavendish**. Despite all the friendly affirmations on their website nobody replied to the numerous emails I sent them in trying to arrange a game. After mentioning this to Nick Leefe at Alwoodley he then very kindly organized for us to play there with a member, Richard Atherton, who was the current Captain of the British Golf Collectors Society.

It was a long drive from Leeds to Cavendish which is located near the town of Buxton. The journey is made longer due to the fact that there is no direct route so you are criss-crossing the countryside. If you study the map you will see there are any number of possible ways to get to Buxton. My advice is to stay on the more major roads by going to Chesterfield and then take the A619 and A6.

Cavendish is rather hilly and, even though I am pretty fit, I still had trouble in keeping up with Richard who is ten years older. The course was very green considering it was mid summer and the rough was thick and quite long in parts of the course.

After two reasonably short par 4's you would expect that the 3rd, a par 4 of only 285 yards, would be something of a pushover. However this is high up on the side of the hill so the fairway slopes from right to left. You need to drive to the right hand side but anything a little too far right will be in long grass.

All of the five par 3's are good with a number of them playing from an elevated tee. This is the case at the pretty fourth hole. It is just 122 yards but in front of the green is a bracken filled burn, at the right is a long bunker and if you are well left you will be in a pond.

The 5th and 6th are two of the longest par 4's at over 400 yards but it is the 7th that I felt was one of the best holes. At 312 yards it should be easy but you need to drive close to the thick line of trees along the right and anything long or left of the green is either bunkered or will run down a bank.

7th hole

Par 3, 4th hole at Cavendish

The par 3, 9th is again played from high above the green. This 139 yard hole has a rating of 10 due to the split level green and the deep gully containing a burn and large shrubs that you must hit over. When you don't know the course then these elevated tees make it difficult to judge distance on the short holes.

The 10th is a tricky par 4 of 422 yards. The danger comes with the shot to the elevated green. Anything short or left is in the winding burn or rough on the upslope in front of the green. This hole has won praise from the American architect Tom Doak. At the par 4, 11th a good long drive over the marker post is essential. The only par 5 at Cavendish is the 14th which is not overly long but there is a double dog-leg left and you play into yet another raised green.

The fifteenth is a deceptively treacherous short hole mainly because of the severe slope, especially at the front of the green. Hitting this green is not the problem, but staying on it is. The sixteenth is an attractive par 4 that plays downhill to a green with good views back to the clubhouse. Be sure to avoid going through the back of this green. And the hardest par 4 is saved for the last hole – 441 yards with an undulating fairway and the second shot played over a steep gully to the green set into the side of the slope.

Above: 16th green with the 18th hole and clubhouse behind
Below: 18th hole from behind the green

Cavendish can play longer than its 5721 yards especially if the fairways are a little heavy. The greens were good with some tricky slopes but don't expect a manicured course here. It is in a pretty setting in the Derbyshire countryside and the clubhouse is perfectly suited to the course.

From Buxton the A6 and A619 will get you to within a few miles of **Lindrick** Golf Club located near the town of Worksop on the A57. Originally known as the Sheffield and District Golf Club, Lindrick

Lindrick's opening hole

began in 1891 with nine holes designed by Tom Dunn. Since then, Herbert Fowler and Fred Hawtree have had a hand in some of the holes.

Lindrick is probably best known as the venue for the 1959 Ryder Cup where the Great Britain & Ireland team defeated the USA for the first time on home soil since 1933. The fairways here have a very firm linksy feel helped by the underlying limestone which keeps the course dry even in winter. The greens were excellent and were also quite firm.

Two good par 4's set the scene at the opening. Both bend left and, in the case of the second hole, the fairway narrows before a green that is quite heavily bunkered. The short third was designed by Herbert Fowler in1920. A memorable hole is the short par 5, 4th that runs downhill to a dell green beside the River Ryton. When I was there the river had more of the proportions of a babbling brook.

The 5th tee is beside the 4th green in what is best described as a grotto with a tall stone wall as the backdrop. This is a tough par 4 of 431 yards with a blind drive up a steep hill. The sixth is a lovely short

Top: 4th green beside the River Ryton
Middle: A solid drive uphill is required at the 5th
Below: Looking back from beside the 5th green (Photo courtesy Julian Maturi/Lindrick GC)

hole with gorse and grassy mounds between tee and green.

Another demanding par 4 (439 yards) follows at the 7th. This Willie Park Jnr. design bends left and has two bunkers at the corner. The par 3's are all good at Lindrick. At the short eleventh the green is raised and there are two bunkers at the right.

You cross the busy road to play holes twelve to seventeen but at least for your return at the eighteenth the club has recently built an underpass walkway. The par 4, 13th is Index 1. It dog-legs left and has bunkers at the corner where you then play uphill to a green which slopes to the front and is guarded by four bunkers. The fifteenth is different in that it has no bunkers.

I found the sixteenth and seventeenth to be two of the weakest holes visually. The par 5,16th could be tricky for big hitters trying to reach the green in two as there is a grassed quarry site at the left of the approach to the green. I'm certain Greg Norman remembers the par 4, 17th. Playing in the last round of the Martini International in 1982 he managed to take 14 shots here. He is quoted as later saying that next time he will take two seven irons and settle for a 5.

Above: 7th at Lindrick
Below: 10th hole from behind the green (Photos courtesy Julian Maturi/Lindrick GC)

The round finishes with a long par 3 of 210 yards uphill to a green raised at the front. There is one bunker short right and a further five at the sides. You should take one more club at this hole. Acclaimed though it is, I did not personally find it to be an engaging par 3 but it does show off the clubhouse very well.

Lindrick is a very honest test of golf with firm gorse lined fairways. It lacks a little in having few real standout holes. The lovely old clubhouse was looking rather tired in places inside and could do with a bit of an upgrade. Interestingly we found exactly the same thing at our next port of call, Notts.

Lindrick's 18th green and clubhouse

Travelling due south on the A60 will get you to Kirkby in Ashfield and nearby the delightful **Notts** Golf Club which is sometimes known as Hollinwell because of the holy well beside the eighth tee. Notts goes right back to 1887 but moved to its present site nine miles north of Nottingham in 1901. Willie Park Jnr. was responsible for most of the initial layout with J H Taylor then modifying the bunkers and in 1902 some course extensions were set out by Tom Williamson.

I must confess that I was eagerly awaiting our game at Notts and I was not disappointed. There are some really good holes with very heathland type fairways punctuated by plenty of heather plus bracken, gorse and broom and, in places such as along the 17th hole, lovely rows of pine trees. Only the greens are watered so the fairways can get a little dry in a warm summer.

After a comfortable opening hole the second is somewhat more challenging at 428 yards from the white tees. The hole plays uphill and bends left presenting a tricky long shot into the green. I am referring to the white tees that were more than enough of a challenge with a total length of 6914 yards. Notts stretches to a very long 7250 yards from the blue championship tees.

The par 5, 3rd runs downhill back to the clubhouse and maybe your best chance for a birdie as two good strikes will get you on or close to the green. Two difficult long par 4's are the 4th (440 yards) and the 7th (404 yards) before you reach the marker stone and the well at the 8th tee.

Some of the holes on the back nine left more of an impression with me. The delightful par 4, 11th runs quite steeply uphill through a valley but the really picturesque part of the course is at the elevated tee of the par 3, 13th. Whilst it measures 198 yards, with the green way below the level of the tee it plays much shorter. There is only a thin slither of a fairway if you are short and the banks of the hills on both sides have long grass, heather and patches

The spectacular par 3, 13th at Notts

The short par 4, 16th at Notts

of gorse. There are also five bunkers around the green so it is very satisfying if you can make par here.

I loved the feel of the last three holes, each of which are very different. At the par 4, 16th you have to decide how much of the heather to take on along the right hand side. As this hole is only 353 yards then a drive down the center of the fairway will still put you in good position for the approach to the raised green with a steep bank and bunkers at the front. The 17th is a gorgeous par 5 that sweeps across the side of a hill with the right hand side featuring heather, then gorse and bracken and further right a massive wall of tall pines.

The eighteenth tee is set high amongst bracken and pines as you look straight down the fairway to the clubhouse. This is a challenging par 4 at 460 yards but thankfully it is downhill. The long second shot needs to avoid the wet area that lies short and left of the green and is easier to see when looking back from the green. There are also bunkers in play for both the drive and the second shot.

Notts was both enjoyable and a very good test of your golfing ability. It was a pity that when we played

Par 5, 17th

here in late July the heather was only just beginning to flower. Some of the holes such as the 2nd, 13th, 16th and 17th would look stunning on a sunny day and the heather in full bloom. My only criticism would be that some of the areas inside the clubhouse looked decidedly tired. Perhaps as a visitor this sort of observation is more apparent than for the members who are there every week.

Just a few miles to the north near the town of Mansfield lies **Sherwood Forest** Golf Club. This is a first class heathland track that should be better known than it is. The greens at Sherwood Forest were very true and were the quickest of any that we had played. Most of the fairways had their share of heather and birch trees. It is a solid 6732 yards from the white tees and has ninety four bunkers that are quite penal on some holes.

After three good par 4's you face the very interesting 183 yard 4th hole which plays downhill to the clubhouse. The green has four generous sized bunkers and slopes away at the front and the right. At the 8th, the second of the par 5's, there is a long carry over heather from the tee and then more heather on the right for the second shot.

The par 3, 10th is a good test with heather, deep rough and bunkers unless you carry to the green. The back nine is the harder of the two, particularly because of the stretch from eleven to fourteen of four par 4's that are well over 400 yards. The thirteenth is rather narrow and, along with the fourteenth, has four bunkers in play for the second strike.

The par 5, 16th is not very long but it plays uphill and is heavily bunkered with three at the bend right and a further six from inside 115 yards of the green. The 400 yard 17th also dog-legs right and has a cross bunker

Above: 1st hole at Sherwood Forest
Below: Sherwood Forest nearing sunset – 18th green at the right and 4th green centre of photo

at 180 and 315 yards. One of the best looking holes is undoubtedly the heather clad eighteenth. The fairway initially slopes to the right and the green is well guarded with four bunkers nearby.

The club also has excellent practice facilities that are located higher up on the course beside the sixteenth fairway. Sherwood Forest is well maintained and has some very interesting holes. I guess this should not come as a surprise given that the course was laid out by Harry Colt and James Braid.

Next on the list is one of the very best inland courses in Britain – **Woodhall Spa**. We headed due east toward Lincoln and the A158 before turning off onto the B1191 to the pretty village that is Woodhall Spa.

The complex comprises two courses and the headquarters of the English Golf Union and is set in a beautiful Site of Special Scientific Interest (SSSI) location. The Bracken Course is rather more recent and is the work of Donald Steel. The **Hotchkin** Course is the reason you want to visit. Originally designed by Harry Vardon in 1905 the course underwent major design changes under Colonel Hotchkin in the 1920's. The end result is a brilliant heathland layout with the largest number of deep bunkers I have ever encountered on a heathland course.

The sandy soil is perfect for golf and provides for springy turf amidst the pines, birch, heather, broom and gorse. The fairways are very tight with misdirected shots penalized either by the numerous bunkers or the profuse heather.

I met up with Richard Latham who is in charge of golf operations at Woodhall Spa. When we visited in late July 2011 he mentioned that it had been the worst year for grass growing in the thirteen years he had been there – a combination of a cold winter followed by a very dry spring. This was barely apparent at Woodhall Spa as the fairways were quite good and the greens were excellent. Richard has written the history of Woodhall Spa Golf Club and was currently working on the histories of Muirfield and Royal County Down.

Apart from the need for accuracy, the Hotchkin also demands some good long hitting as it measures over 7000 yards from the blue tees and is only 160 yards shorter from the white. You are immediately aware of this after playing the second and third holes – both over 400 yards and into the wind the day we played. The approach to the third green is highlighted by the remains of the historic brick tower back and right of the green.

There are only three short holes but they are all very challenging with smallish greens, deep bunkers and thick rough nearby. The 5th is thankfully only 148 yards to the narrow green and cavernous bunkers. If you over club you will be amongst the bracken and gorse.

I think it is wise that handicap limits apply here. Apart from the deep bunkers and penal rough, there are also some rather long carries over heather from the tee

Green at the par 3, 5th at Woodhall Spa

The par 3, 12th is one of the best short holes anywhere in the world

Approach to the 13th green

at a number of holes. At the par 5, 6th for example there is a carry required of 225 yards over heather from the blue tee.

The home nine commences with a terrific par 4 of just 338 yards. Your drive must finish short of the right hand bunker followed by a precisely hit short iron which needs to avoid the shelf at the front of the green and then a number of well positioned bunkers. The 11th is a great par 4 where first you drive through trees and gorse and then you must negotiate the cross bunker complex about 70 yards before the raised green.

The twelfth is the last of the par 3's and has to be one of the toughest holes rated Index 18 you will ever encounter. The green is long and narrow and slopes to the front. The bunkers are extremely penal with the one at the left of the green being 12 feet deep. In 1982, whilst playing a match and being called through by the four in front, both competitors holed out here.

The long par 4, 13th (451 yards) is one of the best on the Hotchkin. There are nasty bunkers on both sides of the fairway for the drive and then an array of more bunkers where your second shot is very likely to land at the front of the green. The sixteenth is another hole with a long carry over heather from the tee.

The home hole is a tough par 5 that usually plays into the prevailing wind. Both sides of the fairway are bunkered and you need to avoid my mistake of being blocked by the large oak tree on the right . If you have played to your handicap at the Hotchkin then you have done well. In summary, this is a really good, well presented, layout and is quite demanding. I would highly recommend the Hotchkin but not for high handicap golfers.

After Woodhall Spa I took the opportunity to head to the coast on the A158 to revisit **Seacroft** a great little links course just out of Skegness. My previous game there was in 2006 which was one of the hottest and driest summers in recent history so I was keen to get some photos with more normal conditions. It is well worth a game if it is links you are seeking – just a pity that you have to go to Skegness which would be one of my least favourite towns in England.

The next leg of our heathland trail was a fairly lengthy drive to just north of Birmingham where we stayed near the town of Rugeley prior to playing Beau Desert, close by the A460 heading south to Cannock.

6th hole at Beau Desert

Beau Desert (Beautiful Wilderness) was once part of the Marquess of Anglesey's estate and is located alongside Staffordshire's Cannock Forest. It is a Herbert Fowler design and bares his trademark cross-bunkers.

You need to start with a solid strike as you drive uphill over a crater full of heather and thick rough. The second is a much longer par 4 where you get an early taste of the cross-bunkers here. The par 3, 3rd hole is slightly downhill and anything short will be in rough, anything wide will find one of the four bunkers and if you are too firm then the green runs off down a slope at the rear.

Index 1 is the par 4, 5th which dog-legs left then heads uphill on a fairway with plenty of slopes. The downhill sixth is a very attractive hole with a fairly tight drive through the trees and lovely views of the surrounding countryside. The par 3, 7th with its large hollow demands that you hit the green with your tee shot.

The 9th is a good short par 4 with a raised green and is followed by a captivating par 3 of 140 yards or just 102 from the yellow visitors tee. The green is very quick and hard to hold as it falls away from the center and there is huge cross-bunker along the front. As was the situation at the par 3, 7th your tee shot is through the pines on both sides.

The 13th tee is another part of the course to take in the surrounding country. The tee amongst the trees looks downhill with the fairway bending a little left. Some good holes follow including the sixteenth, the last of the short holes, which is another green protected by a cross-bunker. Possibly the best is left till last. There are only two par 5's at Beau Desert —the fifteenth which plays long if you miss the fairway or catch the cross-bunker and the shorter eighteenth which runs downhill to the clubhouse. It is not too difficult to make your par at the eighteenth but if you try for the green in two and come up short you will be in

an area of heather and gorse that leads into a hollow just short of the green. The view from the top of the hill looking to the green and clubhouse is something special.

Beau Desert is a must if you are anywhere near the area. The course is well maintained and the rather large greens have some interesting slopes and are excellent quality. The clubhouse was close to the best we had experienced so far on the heathland trip.

South of Beau Desert, and just eight miles north of Birmingham,

Par 3, 10th with its narrow opening and large cross-bunker

Approaching the 18th and clubhouse at Beau Desert

near Sutton Coldfield is **Little Aston**. Set out on 166 acres Little Aston is more of a parkland course with only a few small areas containing heather. It is located in an affluent area and has a very small membership of only around 160.

Presumably they have no reticulation on the fairways as when I was there on the last day of July the course was very dry and the tees and greens, which were excellent, really stood out by comparison. On reflection I am quite surprised that it measures 6704 yards from the middle tees because it felt like a much shorter course. The deceptive length may perhaps be partly attributed to having only the three par 3's.

This is a Harry Vardon design that opened in 1908. With the large number of cross-bunkers I would have readily bet that it was the work of Herbert Fowler. I was somewhat underwhelmed by the opening holes which rely heavily on bunkers to give a degree of difficulty. I still cannot comprehend how the fourth hole can be rated Index 1. It is a par 4 measuring just 317 yards. Admittedly the green is well bunkered and can be quick if you are putting from front to back but other holes such as the second, tenth and eighteenth are much more demanding.

The fifth is the shortest of the par 3's at 161 yards. The difficulty comes from the sloping green and the six bunkers protecting it. The par 3, 9th is long (193 yards) and narrow with three greenside bunkers. One of

Par 3, 9th from behind at Little Aston

the most attractive holes is the par 4, 11th where you must drive over a clump of heather to a fairway which slopes right toward the trees but dog-legs left to a raised green.

The 12th is also a good challenge even though at 485 yards it is a short par 5. Initially you need to miss the hidden bunker at the left and then you must next avoid the pond on the left of the approach and the green itself. Playing to a pin position at the left of the green will test your nerves.

The best of the short holes is the thirteenth. The green is well bunkered with just a narrow entrance. A large tree can be in play if you go right and there are shrubs and trees if you run too far through the back of the putting surface. The fourteenth is a short par 4 but it dog-legs sharply to the right where there are huge cross-bunkers on an angle that are in place to catch your drive. A good drive will give a very real birdie opportunity.

The par 5, 15th is best remembered by the large mounds running across the fairway at the 290 yard mark. The par 4, 16th is tree lined on both sides and has three smallish cross-bunkers in front of the green. The seventeenth has in recent years been modified to include a pond that runs around three quarters of the green. The right hand side where there is one bunker is the only approach that can be made along the ground. I'm not convinced that this pond blends in with the hole and I have a suspicion that quite a few members feel the same way.

The closing hole is a testing par 4 of about 400 yards. The fairway bends to the right with three bunkers placed for the tee shot. You are then confronted with the biggest cross-bunker I have ever seen. It is very wide and is angled

Top: The par 4, 11th is a tight driving hole
Middle: The approach to the 12th green can test your nerves
Bottom: The 13th is the best of the short holes

across the whole of the fairway just in front of the green. The front bunker face is sufficiently high that it blocks part of your view of the green thus making distance judgment a little more difficult.

Little Aston was a pleasant round of golf in quiet surrounds but I had expected a little more. As mentioned in the previous chapter, the practice putting green and garden within is wonderful.

Three more golfing destinations remain that are in the southern end of my central England classification – namely Woburn, Ashridge and Berkhamsted. From the Birmingham region you can travel south on either the M1 or the A5. The lovely village of Woburn is then found by detouring a short distance via the A4012 if exiting the M1 or the A418 if you are exiting the A5. Woburn Village is an absolutely delightful heritage Georgian village that was first recorded as a settlement as far back as 969. In 1145 Cistercian Monks founded the famous Abbey at Woburn. Fire destroyed most of the town in 1724 and it was rebuilt in the Georgian style that remains today.

Woburn Golf Club comprises three magnificent courses and it is purely a matter of personal taste as to which course you prefer. They have all held major events and received much praise from the participants.

The **Duke's** Course opened in 1976 and, like the Duchess which followed two years later, was designed by Charles Lawrie. The land was formerly owned by the Duke of Bedford and was dense woodland. The natural terrain is largely undisturbed which has resulted in a wonderful variety of holes with twists and turns through the mature pines, birch and chestnuts. Many of the greens have a secluded feel as they are set in natural amphitheatres. In the case of all four par 3's on the Duke's you play over a natural depression in the terrain. There is no heather or gorse, just trees and bracken and rhododendrons which save their colours for Spring.

The tee box at the par 5, 1st hole is set to the left where you are faced with a line of trees and then OOB. I seem to recall hitting one of those trees with my opening drive and commenced the day three off the tee! This hole is often used as the eighteenth during tournaments and on one of these occasions Nick Faldo managed to take nine shots here. The pretty par 3, 3rd hole is the cover photo on the scorecard. You hit from an elevated tee over a wall of bracken to a green 100 feet below the level of the tee.

Par 5, 1st hole on the Duke's at Woburn which is often played as the 18th in tournaments

Above and below: Two views of the 4th green. Looking back you can see the twisting nature of the fairway

It is a very hard to judge 134 yards and there is no safe place unless you are on the green which slopes severely to the front. Behind the green is almost impenetrable with bracken and rhododendrons and there are large bunkers on each side.

The par 4, 4th is a wonderful example of one of the many greens set into the upslope at the end of a tree lined valley. Accuracy is not just a necessity from the tee as you will also have to contend with holes such as the fifth where there is a large swale left of the green and the thirteenth where the fairway falls away along the right.

Above: Picture postcard par 3, 3rd
Below: The difficult par 3, 6th

The sixth is the most difficult of the short holes. From the very back tee it measures 207 yards (170 from the yellow) and you are playing over a deep hollow to a raised green with trees close by, especially on the right if you are short. If you are straight but short then your ball will roll down to the foot of the hill. The 7th is a monster par 4 of 464 yards and is rated Index 1. Behind the green is a church and graveyard.

Every hole offers a different challenge. The long par 4, 16th needs a draw from the tee but at the seventeenth you need a slight fade in order to

avoid the trees at the corner of the dog-leg. The final hole is the only shortish par 4 at 356 yards from the white and 322 yellow, however it bends around to the right and pine trees are very much in play on both sides of the fairway.

The thick canopy of trees creates a real feeling of privacy with the solitude often disrupted only by the clatter of a Titleist crashing into a pine tree. Since opening, the Duke's has hosted the Dunlop Masters, British Masters, Ladies Dunhill Classic and the Womens British Open just to name a few events. The Dukes at Woburn is definitely on my list for a return visit.

The **Duchess'** Course is the shortest of the three but is still a healthy 6651 yards from the white (6442 from the yellow tees). Each of the four par 3's is first class and there are many lovely holes that play through avenues of pines. To quote Ian Poulter, the Woburn touring professional, "this hidden gem puts a massive premium on straight hitting".

You get a taste of things to come right from the first hole – a long par 4 which requires you to drive close to the trees on the left followed by a long second strike to a raised green with a large bunker front right. The shot into the long par 3, 2nd needs to be rifle straight to hit the two level green in an amphitheatre setting. The third is a par 4 of only 326 yards but the hole is rated Index 12 so that is something of a warning that it is no pushover. There is an area of rough about 60 yards short of the small green which is angled to the left. The par 5, 4th is not overly long but plays longer due to the dog-leg left which can cause you to run out of fairway unless your drive is a solid draw.

Above: The 13th at the Duke's is a demanding par 4
Below: 18th at the Duke's

You require a well hit shot to be on in regulation at the 203 yard 7th. This narrow hole is lined with trees and anything short will either be deflected off the bank in front of the green or will come to rest in the large bunker at the right. At the eighth you face a near 90 degree dog-leg right so only a well placed drive will give you a look at the green.

There doesn't need to be many fairway bunkers here as the narrow tree lined fairways are tough enough. Index 1 is the long par 4, 14th and is one of the few to feature a fairway bunker – commencing at 214 yards from the tee. The green runs off to a bank at the right so it seems safer to aim left but you must first clear the greenside bunker. The 15th is a dog-leg par 5 where a short drive will leave you blocked by trees. The fairway then slopes left down a hill before rising sharply to a two-tiered green.

The sixteenth is the prettiest and the shortest of the par 3's. You play over a valley to a raised green with two bunkers front right and one that is back left. A poorly hit slice will likely kick right and finish amongst the tall trees. The two remaining holes are par 4's that bend left at the seventeenth and right at the eighteenth.

It is very hard to choose between the Duchess' and the Duke's –they are both really special. On the Duchess in particular you need the courage to try to ignore the trees and still go for your shots – easier said than done!

I have yet to play the **Marquess'** course but managed to have a quick look at some of the holes. It is the longest of the three stretching to 7213 yards from the back tees and is set on 200 acres of mixed woodland featuring pines, spruces, chestnuts and oaks. The fairways are noticeably wider and the greens larger and often with quite big undulations. It did not take long to be acclaimed as, although it only opened in 2000, the British Masters was held there in the following year.

Top: Looking back from behind the green at the par 5, 15th at the Duchess' Course
Above: 18th at the Duchess' Course, Woburn

Par 3, 16th at the Duchess' Course, Woburn

South of Woburn and just off the B4506 and just 40 miles north of London lies **Ashridge**. Although not established till 1932, Ashridge was soon on the golfing map when Henry Cotton won three Open Championships whilst the professional there. Later Alex Hay held that position for twelve years from 1964. The design is attributed equally to C K Hutchinson, Sir Guy Campbell and Colonel Hotchkin of Woodhall Spa fame. The clover leaf design has the advantage of providing the choice of commencing play at the 1st, 10th or 13th holes.

Although it is 6663 yards from the back tees Ashridge is a rather more modest 6145 from the forward tees. It is gently undulating with fairly generous fairways and some good bunkering. The soil provides for excellent golfing turf and in parts this parkland course has something of a heathland feel. The scenery is enhanced by the presence of wild deer and lovely views of the nearby Chiltern Hills.

A fairly gentle start leads to perhaps the prettiest hole at Ashridge, the second, that is appropriately named 'Golden Valley'. You need to avoid the fairway bunkers at the left for your drive and you can then play through the valley with birdie a real chance on this short par 5. The short holes were all noteworthy including the 3rd hole where you play slightly uphill to a green with only a narrow opening between two bunkers.

The fifth is the longest hole and features some very good greenside bunkering. The par 3, 6th measures 207 yards from the back and 174 from the yellow tees. This is a tough hole with a green that borrows right to left and light rough and gorse awaiting a poor shot that is under-clubbed. Similarly at the par 3, 8th you will find rough or gorse with anything short. A feature of the par 4, 9th is the downhill second shot to the very tricky green.

Above: 14th green at Ashridge
Below: Playing to the 18th green; the equally tricky 9th green is behind

The eleventh is another good short hole where the main danger is being anywhere right amongst the trees. The twelfth requires a tight line from the tee preferably a little to the right for the best angle into the green. The short par 5, 17th presents a birdie prospect but watch for the tricky green. The 18th is a very good finishing hole of 433 (400 from forward tee) yards. The fairway runs to the right so your drive needs to avoid the two bunkers on that side and then you play downhill to a long and narrow two-tiered green with a deep bunker on both sides. The hole plays somewhat harder when the flag is located on the upper level.

The lovely 2nd hole at Ashridge is appropriately called 'Golden Valley'

My wife and I had the pleasure of playing Ashridge in 2011 with the Captain, Bill McCreadie (and his dog). This is an enjoyable course that seems to set a good balance between fun and degree of difficulty. The greens were good and the ambience in the relatively new clubhouse was very friendly.

Just a few miles south and somewhat hidden away is the lovely heathland layout, **Berkhamsted** which has its origins back as far as 1890. The course of today reflects upgrades made from 1923 to 1926 by James Braid. Sitting outside the clubhouse, it gave the impression of being a little hilly because of a fairly dramatic view across to the 9th tee. In fact it is quite flat apart from this one hole. Berkhamsted is located in a pleasant wooded area and will punish wayward shots with plenty of bracken, heather, gorse and long grass. An unusual characteristic of the course is that there are no sand bunkers. They have more than compensated by having fairway mounds and grassy banks and hollows particularly around the greens.

A fairly easy opening is followed by a good little par 3 of 156 yards. If you are short then there is plenty of thick rough and heather as well as a May tree that stands front and left of the green. Two smaller trees guard the left and right edges of the green approach area. The drive at the par 4, 3rd needs to carry 180 yards to miss the heather and must avoid another May tree at 120 yards.

Berkhamsted's par 3, 2nd

This is what awaits you at the 9th tee

Index 1 is the 459 yard 4th. Watch for the pond at the 220 yard mark on the right. A number of the longer holes, for example the fourth, six, seventh and eighteenth, have cross rough usually at the approach area to the green and grassy mounds and hollows appear on most holes.

The par 4, 9th is very memorable because of the view from the tee but the drive is really not as hard as it first appears. The high tee overlooks a valley full of shrubs and bracken and is followed by a shot over the edge of the heather along the left side of the fairway.

The 10th is a long par 3 but you can run the ball on to the green featuring grassy mounds along the right and back. Berkhamsted's longest hole is the 11th (568 yards from the back) which has gorse on both sides of the fairway and a heathery, grassy hollow about 80 yards short of the target.

The thirteenth and fourteenth are both par 4's of about the same length. The fourteenth is certainly a bit different with a bitumen road that carries local traffic running across the fairway just in front of the tee. There is an area of bracken and gorse then large grassy mounds before the fairway proper. A slight fade is needed from the tee shot. The long 16th and par 4, 18th are good finishing holes. Avoid the area of bracken, gorse and heather as you approach the final green which has its share of grassed hollows along the sides.

Berkhamsted was a pleasant course to play. When I was there in August the fairways were fairly dry but, despite that, the bracken was profuse near the edge of many fairways. I'm told that the greens are normally very good. I could believe that but unfortunately they were being scarified the day we played. Probably the only negative factor is that you have to cross over a road twice as well as playing over one at the fourteenth.

Watch for the cars at the 14th tee

Broken ground, as seen in front of the 18th green, is used on a number of holes at Berkhamsted.

SOUTH EAST ENGLAND
"If it's not a baffy, it's a niblick"

Playing the best of the heathland courses around London in August when the heather is in full bloom has to be one of the most exhilarating golfing experiences you could ever want. Add in the springy well drained fairways and often magnificent stands of Scots Pines, birches and oaks then this is nature at its sublime best.

Right from our first adventure in this area (which was at The Berkshire) in early August it was as though the heather had, virtually overnight, blossomed in full glory. Pretty as it is, there is a real art in spotting where your ball has landed when you hit into a sea of heather. I noticed signs at many courses, particularly at Hankley Common, warning of the dangers of adders in the heather. Before I saw the first such sign I have to admit to being totally unaware of their presence but, despite trampling through plenty of heather, I am yet to see one.

It appeared to me that there are basically two different types of heather, one rather softer than the other. Whilst it is mostly a rich pink colour, at courses such as Walton Heath the heather takes on a purple hue – particularly around the bunkers.

Apart from learning the knack of finding your ball, you also need to develop the skill of exiting the heather. When we played at Walton Heath we met up again with our friend Ken Macpherson who was the professional there for over thirty years. Ken accompanied us during our round on the New Course and related to me one of the lovely sayings of the great James Braid. Braid was the first professional at Walton Heath and had a remarkable history of 46 years of service from 1904 till his death in late1950. Braid would be heard saying to the members, "if it's not a baffy, it's a niblick".

For the benefit of younger readers, in the days of hickory clubs a baffy was the name given to a 5 wood and a niblick was a lofted iron. What Braid was saying is that if your ball is sitting on top of the heather then you need to sweep it off the top with a 5 wood but if it is sitting down low, as is usually the case, then don't get greedy just get it back on the fairway with say, a 9 iron. From my own experience I found that where the heather was thick then the best method was to play a sand wedge off the back foot and hit with a downward stroke. The first rule is to get back on to the fairway so you have to accept the 'penalty'.

The Berkshire is the most recent of the three great thirty six hole complexes in the Windsor and Virginia Water area. It may not have the profile of its near neighbours but it is not far behind Sunningdale and I personally prefer it to Wentworth. The day I was there it had rained during the morning and lightly for our first twelve holes but being mid summer I was surprised at how much water lay on the fairways and in the bunkers. Fortunately, the rain cleared late in the day and I was able to get some photographs that would do justice to this lovely layout. Despite the rain the greens were very true and were surprisingly fast. Both the Red and the Blue courses date from 1928 and are the work of Herbert Fowler.

Par 3, 7th on the Red Course

The Berkshire **Red Course**, at about 6400 yards, is the longer and slightly hillier of the two. It was not until after the round was completed that I realized the unusual design feature where there are six par 3's, six par 4's and six par 5's.

Opening hole, The Berkshire, Red Course

The opening is a lovely par 5 with ample heather in front of the tee and a wall of mature trees on either side. The fairway narrows a little toward the green and you need to watch for the burn half way from the tee.

Index 1 is the par 4, 4th of approximately 400 yards. The second shot is uphill where a steep bank and large bunker are short and left of the green. At the short fifth you play downhill but it is hard to see the three greenside bunkers. The 6th is an excellent short par 4 with a severe dog-leg to the right.

The 10th is a superb short hole

The majestic 17th is the longest hole on the Red Course

The par 3, 7th is a lovely looking hole but is quite challenging being 195 yards in length with one large bunker and heather waiting for any thing short. Trees are very close to the left.

In springtime the greenside surrounds of the eighth are a blaze of colour from the rhododendrons. You need a fade from the tee before the uphill approach to the green. One of the real standout holes is the uphill par 3,10th which plays 188 yards from the white tees or 148 from the yellow. Anything short and right will disappear into a sea of heather and long and right will kick down a steep gully. Beautiful it may be but this can be a treacherous hole so you are best to aim for the left side of the green.

Par 3, 18th

There are some very attractive holes toward the end of the back nine, particularly the short par 5, 15th, the long tree lined par 3, 16th and the par 5, 17th which sweeps right through the trees and with ample heather waiting if you cut too much off the corner. The slightly anticlimactic closing hole is a par 3 that plays up a fairly steep hill to a tiered green. You can't see much from the tee except for acres of heather and two greenside bunkers.

I can't think of one weak hole on the Red. The holes that stay in your mind are the first five of the wonderful par 3's.

The **Blue Course** is slightly shorter and flatter than the Red and very nearly as good. It is perhaps a pity that the first has to be played as the opening hole. It looks spectacular and is close to the hardest par 3 you are ever likely to play. In fact, when I first saw it I assumed it was a short par 4. Playing 217 yards from the back tee (211 yellow) and uphill over heather as far as you can see there are also two reasonable sized bunkers. The best line is to aim for the front left of the green. This not a hole you want to take on after a big lunch or a rush to the tee after being caught in traffic.

There are a few birdie opportunities on the front nine where there are some shorter par 4's such as the second and par 5's like the 3rd which measures only 475 yards. The par 3, 4th is pretty hole with long grass and heather if you are short and big rhododendrons at the right.

The 6th is a testing par 5 (526 yards) where a stream runs across at about 300 yards and then continues for quite a way on the left. The par 5, 11th has a similar scenario with its burn. The 7th is an interesting par 4 that has a big dog-leg left whilst the very short par 4, 9th plays uphill and has a narrow opening to the green.

The 10th is a gorgeous par 3 of 232 yards (191 yellow) that plays slightly downhill. Trees are close to the line down the right and there is danger by way of thick rough at the left. The par 4, 12th is another

The wonderful opening par 3 at The Berkshire, Blue Course

pretty hole where the green is tiered with the front being higher. The closing five holes are all par 4's of reasonable length.

The courses are both excellent and the clubhouse at The Berkshire is very nice but I have to say that the people in there did not seem overly friendly.

I have reviewed the remaining courses in the order in which I played them so they are not necessarily in strict location order. Having said that, only Royal Ashdown Forest and West Sussex required any lengthy drive from our base at Tilford in Surrey.

South of London on the A22 just beyond East Grinstead in Sussex is **Royal Ashdown Forest**. There are two courses here, each over 100 years old. The West Course is more woodland but it is the more revered Old Course that you want to play. Royal Ashdown Forest has a very old fashioned natural feel, no doubt partly due to the fact that it is protected by Acts of Parliament. This beautiful area was the inspiration for stories of Winnie the Pooh and his forest friends by A A Milne. "The forest will always be there… and anybody who is Friendly with Bears can find it." [1]

Par 4, 2nd at Royal Ashdown Forest

A solid drive is needed at the first where you can easily finish up on the 18th fairway which runs alongside at the right. The 2nd is a lovely down hill par 4 but the first real challenge is at the 510 yard downhill par 5, 5th. Your third shot will be from a downhill lie to a green located just ten yards behind a stream.

The 6th, 'The Island', is only 125 yards but trouble is never far away (just ask my wife). A stream runs in front of and then alongside the left of the two-tiered green that is forty yards long. The sigh of relief

1. The House at Pooh Corner A. A. Milne (first published 1928)

Par 3, 6th 'The Island'

Surrounds of the 8th green illustrate why they don't need bunkers at Royal Ashdown Forest

as you hit the green can soon be replaced by the anguish of a three putt.

The par 5, 8th is on higher ground with a sloping fairway and broken ground with mounds and heather in front of the green. The short ninth plays longer as it is up a steep heather clad incline. The eleventh and twelfth are two fabulous holes played from high tees. The 11th is a monster par 3 of 249 yards downhill from a tee that is almost the highest point anywhere in the county and provides stunning views across to the North Downs. I must confess to having no idea of the distance to carry the heather and even

Above: The long par 3, 11th
Below: Clubhouse at Royal Ashdown Forest as seen from the 1st fairway

less idea of what club to use. I can tell you it was very exhilarating to see my strike with the driver finish just 5 feet from the hole. Bigger hitters would be advised to use no more than 3 wood unless they are into the wind.

The par 5, 12th is a brilliant hole that also plays downhill to a fairway that will run your ball from right to left. There is a long carry over heather and you need to keep your drive to the right as anything even a little left will either run into heather or finish amongst the birch trees.

The par 4, 13th plays up a steep hill over an intimidating bracken filled hollow in front of the tee. After the steep climb there is quite a long walk along a country lane through some woodland to a lovely little downhill par 3. Anything short is in rough or heather and the green can be hard to hold as it slopes away from you. The main danger at the par 4, 15th is the area just short of the green where there are mounds and heather blocking your path.

The two finishing holes are both on hilly terrain. The 17th is a very long par 4 of 486 yards but is downhill and can be reached with a good drive and an iron. The green is a narrow target set

Above: The 13th from behind
Below: Looking back from the elevated 18th green

into the side of the hill on the right. The 18th requires a well hit drive to clear some horrible thick rough at the bottom of the hill adjacent to the clubhouse. The lie of the land will tend to kick your ball further right so a draw is the best option. The green is a steep climb but from there the views are memorable.

I really enjoyed Royal Ashdown Forest but it was rather different to what I had expected. It is very hilly and this was more pronounced by the fact that we seemed to play into a headwind on most of the holes that were uphill. The lack of bunkers is more than compensated for by the heathery mounds, bracken and slopes. I would not recommend this course for women who are not of a reasonable standard as there were some tough carries from the ladies tees. I would have liked to have been there the following week when Royal Ashdown Forest was the venue for the British Ladies Amateur.

We were made to feel genuinely welcome which was in keeping with the lovely natural but unpretentious surrounds.

Time did not permit, but I have been told that **Crowborough Beacon** just a little further south on the A26 is an interesting course with some similarities to Royal Ashdown Forest and is well worth a game.

Our next two destinations were back in the heart of the Surrey/Berkshire sandbelt. Our good friend from Scotland, Duncan Martin, had tipped us off that Keith Maxwell, the Scottish pro at **Sunningdale**, was rather fond of shortbread. So our first task there was to deliver some home made shortbread made back in Australia by my Scottish born wife, Irene. We played as a fourball with a friend of mine from Commonwealth, who lives part of the year at Bray near Ascot, and Jamie Sears a well known member at Sunningdale. Apart from being an entertaining golfing partner it was good to play a course such as Sunningdale with a member given that there are some long carries over heather and dog-legs through heavily wooded areas. His local knowledge was invaluable, even if he couldn't always carry out his own instructions.

If you have never been to Sunningdale then please take my word for it – both courses are sensational from both the golfing and the scenic aspect. This is clearly the premier thirty six hole complex anywhere in Britain. What I thought added to the day was that the atmosphere was very friendly and not somewhat reserved as I had anticipated.

The Old Course opened in 1901 and was originally designed by Willie Park Jnr. The New Course, which is a little more open and hillier, dates from 1923 and is primarily the work of Harry Colt who was also the club's first Secretary.

We arrived at about 8am on a fine but cool and cloudy Tuesday morning and I was rather surprised as to how few cars were in the car park. The greens on the Old Course had been cored and sanded the previous day! Perhaps it was serendipity but it meant that we pretty much had Sunningdale to ourselves, so much so that after playing the first ten holes of the New, at our host's suggestion, we then switched to the back nine of the Old Course. Playing there for the first time I have to admit that the holes all seemed to fit in seamlessly and at no time did it feel as though we were combining two different courses.

1st hole marker for the yellow tees on the Old Course

We were handed cards for the white tees. You can add on about three hundred yards for the back tees but the test from the white felt more than adequate. The **Old Course** begins with an interesting par 5 of 492 yards. The bumps in the middle of the fairway are from an iron age burial site. A long par 4 is then followed by a tricky little par 4 of just 292 yards and yet is rated Index 12. At the fifth you need to watch for the pond that is in play for the second shot. The fairway, like so many at Sunningdale, is bordered by heather and trees and has two bunkers before reaching the green which has another four to protect it.

Above: Looking back to the 10th tee at Sunningdale
Below: The 12th is rated the hardest on the Old Course

One of the very best on the Old is undoubtedly the long par 4, 10th (459 yards) where you can open your shoulders at the elevated tee. The shorter eleventh is also a fine hole where you must avoid a nasty bunker with the drive and then watch for more around the green at the right and heather everywhere.

Index 1 is nowhere near the longest par 4 but the 12th (416 yards) has thick heather on both sides and a very demanding second shot uphill to a green with a small entrance, a heathery mound on the right and a heather and gorse filled bank back left.

The par 3, 15th is 222 yards even from the white. There are two bunkers and plenty of heather if you aren't on the green. The sixteenth is something of a quandary for the average golfer. A par 4 of 423 yards, there is a series of cross bunkers short of the already well bunkered green so you may have to lay up which almost makes this a par 5.

Sunningdale – Mother Nature at its best

Above : 16th – plenty of heather and bunkers
Below: Looking down the 17th and 18th of the Old Course to the clubhouse

The view from the seventeenth tee is majestic as you look over the two last holes towards the big oak tree and the grand clubhouse. The closing holes are solid par 4's. At the eighteenth the fairway will kick your tee shot to the right where a bunker awaits. The second shot is over a cross bunker to a green that includes a bunker provided by the Luftwaffe in 1940. It was felt that the bomb crater improved the hole so it remains there.

The **New Course** commences with a pretty tough par 4 measuring 451 yards. The fairway slopes to the right at the beginning so a solid strike with a slight draw is ideal. At the short second the two-tiered green can be tricky but the real standout par 3 has to be the much photographed 5th. In front of the elevated green is a steep slope with a bunker and thick heathery outcrops. Two more bunkers are at the right and if you are long you will be down a steep bank or caught up in heather at the back left of the green. If you land on the first third of the green surface you are certain to run back down the slope. The hole plays at 167 yards from the white tees and 183 from the back. Harry Colt might just as well have signed his name on the green – it has his unmistakable design characteristics.

Above: 18th green with its extra bunker courtesy of the Luftwaffe
Below: Harry Colt's much acclaimed par 3, 5th at the New course

The par 5, 6th is a difficult short three shotter with its dog-leg, burn and massive amounts of heather. The attractive par 4, 8th rises uphill with trees close to the right hand side and heather everywhere. The par 3, 10th is long and has trees close by along the right and nasty bunkers at the left and front right of the green. Once you have putted out you can experience the lovely food at the half way house. Among the closing holes is the tough par 3 at the 14th and a very difficult par 4 at the 15th which dog-legs around a pond. It pretty much goes without saying that nearly every hole has large amounts of heather which, on the occasion of my visit, was long and thick.

Both course were beautifully presented. The greens are quite large and were very good based on those we played that had not been cored and sanded. The bunkers were first class, many with thick heather eyebrows. Sunningdale is not for poor standard golfers. There are long carries over the heather for the men and some that were extremely long for the average lady golfer which is probably why they have visitors handicap limits of 18 for men and 24 for women. I can't wait to play Sunningdale again!

New Course, par 4, 8th

At the end of our heathland journey from Leeds to London encompassing 30 courses it was interesting that my wife and I each voted for the same club as the venue for our most enjoyable day's golf. And the winner was… **St George's Hill** in Weybridge on the A245 just south of Sunningdale.

Harry Colt's design opened in 1913 and by 1929 St George's Hill was extended to thirty six holes. In 1920 the original clubhouse was largely destroyed by a fire that started in the thatched roof. Following on from the effects of the War, by 1946 a lack of funds and a falling membership led to the second course being reduced to nine holes and the surplus land sold for housing.

To access the golf club you drive through a gated community (John Lennon's all white house is here) to a stately clubhouse set on the side of a treed and heather clad hill that overlooks much of the course. This is a really magnificent housing estate and at no stage do the houses intrude onto the course. The Red and Blue

The beautiful opening hole at St George's Hill

nines make up the main course with the shorter remaining holes known as the Green nine.

I have played nearly 300 courses in the UK and Ireland and St George's Hill certainly gets my award as having the most beautiful opening hole. From an elevated tee you drive over heather to a valley and from there the green is high up in a beautiful treed setting. To the right of the approach is a high bank with heather along the sides. Provided you hit an accurate second shot, this hole is not as hard as it looks.

But the 458 yard par 4, 2nd is a tough hole which starts with a semi bind drive. A small stream cuts across the fairway about two thirds of the way and then the second shot is over a small valley with a bunker 50 yards short right and another left side of the green. The 3rd is a long but straight forward par 3, well bunkered at the left. The short par 4, 4th features a distinctive triangular bunker formation in front of the green. The fifth requires a precise drive which must carry heather and then avoid two bunkers at the left.

A blocked tee shot will either finish in heather or amongst the pines. Before you reach the green there is a rather large cross-bunker complex to be negotiated.

Index 1 is the long par 4, 6th (468 yards) that requires a long carry over the heather and the 7th, which is about the same length, is a par 5. The eighth and ninth are each memorable holes. The par 3, 8th plays over a deep valley with heather clumps – don't be short on this hole as there are also three bunkers set into the side of the hill and another to the left. The 9th tee looks toward the lovely clubhouse. Three bunkers and

Top: 5th hole
Above: Par 3, 8th from behind the green

9th hole, 18th green and clubhouse

then a pond will collect anything pulled left. The shot into the green is uphill making distance difficult to judge. The green has a steep slope at the front so anything a little short may roll back down the hill.

Apart from the 6th, the par 4, 10th is the only other hole at St George's Hill that has a long carry over heather at the tee. The difficulty in playing here for the first time is that you can't tell from the tee exactly how far the heather continues over the hill.

Above: The tricky short 11th
Bottom: 16th hole

The very short 11th (110 yards) is another great Harry Colt par 3. The deep valley makes judging distance all the more difficult. Trees are close by at the right and heather and

Par 4, 17th St George's Hill

bunkers are waiting. Probably the only place to miss where you still might scramble a par is to the left of the green. The par 4, 12th plays to a green in a very pretty woodland setting where you get one of the few glimpses of one of the expensive houses beside the course. The last par 3, the 14th, is somewhat more bland despite the pond that is well in in front of the green.

I really liked the last three holes, all par 4's but each totally different. The tree-lined sixteenth is well bunkered and is very picturesque, the seventeenth plays down hill with trees close to the left of the fairway and the final hole hugs the side of the hill below the clubhouse. When playing to the eighteenth green you have the thick heather bordering the tenth on your right and at the left, lower down, is the ninth green.

The day may have been a little wet but the course was a joy to play and the stately clubhouse was equally welcoming. I can recommend St George's Hill as one of those definite 'must play' golfing experiences.

If you want to experience heather by the acre then it is **Hankley Common** that you need to visit. It is part of a SSSI Site on Tilford Road which runs off the A287 south of Farnham. If you are approaching from London then you would take one of the minor roads after first using the A3.

The whole countryside around Tilford has large expanses of heather. We spent 10 days based at a B & B near Tilford so on several balmy evenings we took the opportunity to walk along the bridle path that takes you past the 11th hole and the famous Atlantic Wall referred to in Chapter 4. Beside the entrance to the car park is the highly recommended Duke of Cambridge Hotel.

Top: Par 3, 2nd at Hankley Common
Middle: A well placed drive is required at the 5th
Above: Don't be short at the 7th
Right: Military exercises are still held in the area beyond the bridle path near the Atlantic Wall and the 11th hole

The first four holes at Hankley Common are a little circuit of their own that return to the clubhouse. After a solid par 4 start, the 2nd is a delightful short hole of 166 yards that is in amongst the pines. Heather and a bunker are in front of the green, a grassy hollow is at the right, trees are close by on the left and if you are too strong you will be in the bracken.

From the 5th it is more of an out and back layout. This hole is a good dog-leg left with a bunker and then trees at the left hand corner. All four of the short holes are first class at Hankley Common, none better though than the seventh. Being uphill it plays longer than its 183 yards and with all the heather you cannot afford to be short. Bunkers guard both sides of the entrance to the green.

The par 5, 8th has a slightly raised tee from where you get a good look at the challenge ahead. If you are a little offline with the drive there is a bunker that is hard to see on each side of the start of the fairway beyond the heather and then the fairway narrows at the point where a ditch runs across.

Index 1 is the long par 4, 10th at 423 yards from the white tees but a much tougher 477 from the back. The par 3, 11th requires a carry of about 170 yards before the apron to the slightly raised green where, just like the 7th, a bunker lies at each side of the front entrance. Even from the white tees this is a long par 3 at 216 yards. It virtually goes without saying that at Hankley Common if you miss the fairway you will be in heather and if you miss it badly then you will be amongst the trees.

The par 4, 14th plays through pines and has four large bunkers as you approach the green. A big dog-leg left and then a tricky green awaits you at the short par 4, 15th. The short 16th appears straightforward but it can be a dangerous hole. It plays slightly uphill with heather all the way to the well bunkered green, the front of which slopes back to the small apron. Left is definitely not the place to be as here you will have to deal with gorse and birch trees as well as the heather.

Left top: Hankley Common's par 3, 11th
Left: The short 15th features a big dog-leg left

Hankley Common's 14th hole

The last two holes are par 4's that provide for a cracking finish. The tree lined seventeenth bends left at the bridle path. At the eighteenth you must get a good drive away so as to have any chance of hitting and holding the green that has a deep grassy ditch all the way across the front. Any ball that lands short and right will probably have a bed of heather as its last resting place.

Hankley Common has a lovely old fashioned feel. It has been around since 1897 and has been eighteen holes since James Braid's work of 1923 and 1924. The front nine has a more open heathland feel from the third hole onwards whereas the back nine often plays through conifers on both sides of the fairway. Greens and bunkers were very good and the course is easy walking. Despite the huge amounts of heather there are only one or two holes where the carry is a bit tough for ladies.

Above: The 16th is another very good par 3
Below: 18th green and clubhouse at Hankley Common

The clubhouse and meals were also very good which may be part of the reason why Hankley Common is usually pretty busy. You are hard to please if you don't enjoy a day at this lovely quiet location.

Situated in very close proximity along the A322 and A324 in Surrey are the famous 3 W's – West Hill, Woking and Worplesdon. I could have added a fourth – Wisley which is just a mile or two east of Woking.

You can only play The Wisley with a member so from that perspective it was never on my playlist but I did have a very quick look at it. The twenty seven hole complex was designed by Robert Trent Jones Jnr. and opened in 1991. There are numerous water hazards and, compared to the courses I had been playing, the fairways looked lush and almost over watered. I was in England to play the best of the heathland courses so I will admit to having no great desire to play an 'Americanised' course even if it is well conditioned.

I was particularly keen to play **West Hill** since there is a reciprocity agreement with Commonwealth, my home club in Melbourne. This is a very pretty course with beautiful stands of Scots Pines and plenty of heather. The strategic nature of many of the holes makes it play longer than its yardage of about 6350 from the white and 6028 from the yellow tees with a par of just 69. West Hill was designed in 1907 by Cuthbert Butchart, a Scottish professional from Carnoustie, who was a renowned club maker and became the club's first professional.

The round begins with two good par 4's where you need to be accurate from the tee and avoid the bunkers. The 3rd is a very good par 4 which starts with a semi blind drive from a raised tee. As you head towards the green the ground tends to kick your ball left where a stream can be in play.

3rd tee West Hill

One of the standout features of these heathland courses is the high quality of the short holes. West Hill has some first class par 3's – none better than the 193 yard 4th. You hit over a slight hollow with a burn and heather clumps beyond to a very well bunkered green. Left is the best side if you are going to miss the green.

The par 5, 5th is made longer by the drive being uphill and the 6th is tricky due to the cross bunkers about 50 yards short of the green. The par 4, 8th is a superb looking hole with stands of pines and great bunkering before you reach the slightly raised green.

The tenth and eleventh are very challenging par 4's, especially when you are playing here first time. Ten has a very tight drive and at the eleventh there is some broken ground and the burn is in play on the undulating fairway. The 12th is a very short par 4 but it is very heavily bunkered in the approach area and the green is severely two-tiered. The par 3, 13th showcases the wonderful bunkering at West Hill. A ditch runs in front of the green that is even more protected because of the high face on the front bunkers. If you over club then beware as OOB is at the rear.

The par 3, 15th is 211 yards from the white (182 yellow) and requires a precise tee shot. Trees are close to the right and there is heather if you don't finish on the green or in a bunker and the green is not

Top left: Par 3, 4th
Middle left: Wonderful bunkering at the par 4, 8th
Left: Looking back to the tee at the 17th

West Hill's closing hole provides for a challenging second shot on this testing par 4

easy as it has a hogs back in the center. The par 5, 17th requires a solid drive over acres of heather. The eighteenth is a great finishing hole. At 440 yards (418 yellow) you are faced with the problem of a long second shot that must clear the huge cross-bunkers but not run through the undulating green where the clubhouse and OOB is very close. For a visitor this shot is even more daunting when there are people sitting outside the clubhouse, seemingly in your line of fire.

I suspect that West Hill should be rated a little higher. My only criticism would be that the greens were a little slow and bumpy but, in fairness, a friend of mine from Commonwealth played there recently and he said the greens were fine.

Nearby, the construction of a course to be known as **Worplesdon** was taking place at the same time as West Hill. As the club's history explains, there was some confusion as to who exactly was responsible for the design. Colt was mentioned and another contemporary article claimed it was Willie Park Jnr. with J F Abercromby designing the bunkers. The centenary history is adamant that Abercromby was the guiding hand. Apparently this was done as a labour of love. Then, as a result of its success, 'Aber' joined the golf course architect firm which became Fowler, Abercromby, Simpson & Croome.

Worplesdon Golf Club is also synonymous with Roger and Joyce Wethered and the Worplesdon Mixed Foursomes which commenced in 1921. The Wethereds were certainly two of the finest golfers of their time. Roger won the British Amateur in 1923 and was beaten in the final by Bobby Jones in his Grand Slam year, 1930. In 1921 he tied for first in The Open at St Andrews, before losing in the play-off, after incurring a penalty stroke in the third round for accidentally standing on his ball. Sister Joyce won the English Ladies Championship five years in a row from 1920 and was British champion four times often competing against the great Cecil Leitch.

The first at Worplesdon is perfect as an opening hole. A medium length par 4 uphill, all the dangers are set out before you —heather if you are short, bunkers at the left and a bunker beside a large tree for the blocked shot to the right. The next two holes are good par 4's that run at right angles to the first. The lovely uphill par 3, 4th then plays back to the clubhouse. A deep bunker guards the front right with another further behind. A duffed tee shot will find heather and a pull to the left is heading for the chestnut tree. If you over-club then your ball may finish in a patch of heathery bank at the back.

1st hole at Worplesdon

4th hole from behind the green at Worplesdon

The fifth is a great looking par 4 where you drive slightly uphill with the fairway bending right. Two bunkers and two hollows guard the green. To quote Noel Stephens in the club history: "The banking and subtle contours of the green were, surely, the work of Willie Park Jnr."[1].

The par 3, 7th is a fine hole with deep bunkering and a two-tiered green. Whilst the 8th is only a medium length par 4 you need to watch for the bunker and pine trees at the inside corner of the gentle dog-leg left. The ninth was redesigned around 1970 and is a demanding fairly narrow driving hole with a pond at the right before it curves to the right.

The tenth is the signature hole at Worplesdon. A par 3 of just 139 yards, it is all carry over a large pond with a tiny apron in front of the green set among the trees and rhododendrons all of which are very close by.

The par 5, 11th is a wonderful example of a three shotter requiring precise hitting to avoid the fairway bunkers. The 12th is a shorter par 5 that dog-legs sharply to the right. There are pine trees on the right hand side with three fairway bunkers at the corner. The green is narrow and has a nasty high heathery mound with a steep bank on the left side of the green. Another good short hole awaits you at the thirteenth. From a slightly raised tee you play over heather to a green almost encircled by bunkers.

Above: Worplesdon's signature par 3, 10th
Below: The dog-leg at the 12th

Index 1 is the very long par 4, 14th at 452 yards from the white but somewhat changed for the yellow tees being 74 yards shorter. The par 3, 16th plays longer than its 183 yards being uphill to a plateau green. You are probably worse off in the heathery banks rather than the bunkers in front of the green.

[1] *"Worplesdon Golf Club, The first 100 years: 1908 to 2008"* Noel Stephens

The 13th is almost an island green

How well I remember the long par 4, 18th. My friendly match with Bill McCreadie was all square at this point. The fairway is reasonably wide but a safe shot to the right leaves you with a difficult line over bunkers at the front right of a green that is angled to the fairway. There is a hollow to the left and anything straight but long can run down a steep bank that leads to OOB by way of a path beside the clubhouse. We both had similar shots to the green. I played safe to the front left of the green but poor Bill hit his second too well and the hard ground did the rest. I wonder how many matches at Worplesdon have been lost in the same manner?

Worplesdon is probably a wee more challenging than West Hill especially with the interesting swales on some of the greens. It is a charming wooded heathland experience but with not as much heather as some of the courses nearby. The greens were very good as was the rest of the course conditioning but having to cross Bagshot Road twice was a bit of a negative. The clubhouse was a little tired looking in places but the patio area outside is a delightful setting.

At a time when most people thought of heathland as not having any benefits, Tom Dunn was something of a trailblazer and in 1893 at **Woking** laid out one of the first courses to be built on the heath.

It poured with heavy rain all morning on the August day of our booking which was for around noon. Apart from my wife and myself there were only two other people in the bar, such was the bleak outlook. As happened frequently on the heathland trip, we commenced with the rain easing and after three holes the sun shone for the rest of the day. As testimony to the quality of Woking, the fairways were quick to lose their surface water and the greens still ran at a good speed.

The 1st is a very short par 4 but don't make the mistake of running through the green. In the rain the par 3, 2nd was something of an uphill slog. The third hole dog-legs right around the side of a hill. At this point I will admit to feeling a little disappointed by the layout. However, from the par 4, 4th Woking takes on the heathland experience I had hoped for. The fourth runs straight with the railway line and OOB along the right. The decision you have to make is whether to play safe or take the attacking line to the right of the bunker that is nearly in the middle of the fairway.

The fifth bends a little right after you hit over some heather and the brook. Too far left with the drive may see you blocked by an oak. A large bank is short and right of the tiered green. For me the best hole at Woking is the par 4, 6th rated Index 1. The fairway runs beautifully down to the green with the brook running in front, but hard to notice first time. Shorter hitters may need to lay up . There is plenty of heather plus bunkers on both sides of the fairway.

The par 3, 7th (161 yards) is slightly uphill over heather with mounded bunkers on each side of the green. At the long par 4, 8th the fairway sweeps right after you have driven over a stream and plenty of heather. A cluster of bunkers short of the green will make you think about whether you lay up or try for the green. I found the 9th to be a very tough par 4 at 446 yards from the white tees and 470 from the back. There is heather well and truly in play for your drive which must be followed by a second shot uphill from the corner where the left dog-leg commences. The plateau green has a significant left to right slope.

7th hole at Woking

At the par 4, 11th you again drive over heather and then the hole bends to the right where a bunker has been cleverly sited. Woking is a thinking person's course and at the par 4, 12th unless you hit a very good drive you must decide if you can carry the three bunkers in front of the green. The back nine seems to have much more heather than the earlier holes. The fourteenth is the first of the two back to back three shot holes. It bends beautifully to the right with a sea of heather along this side and then you are confronted by a wall of

Top: Woking's 4th hole
Above: The par 4, 6th is the photo on the scorecard

heather clad bunkers angled across the front of the green in front of the clubhouse that is very close by. Your initial reaction is that this should be the finishing hole.

The par 3, 16th is only 156 yards with no undulations but the mental hazard comes in the form of the long pond full of rather healthy sized eels that runs to within about fifteen yards of the green. A bunker lies front right and another center left. The last hole, a par 4 of 351 yards, is intriguing. The hole dog-legs right at about the point where you are playing your second shot. The first part of the fairway slopes to the right where there is heather. If your drive finishes even a little right then your shot into the green is played toward the two

Above: Well placed bunker at the 11th
Below: The 14th green is hidden between the bunkers and the clubhouse

Par 3, 16th and a pond full of eels

bunkers and large pond at the right. If you err on the cautious side and your second strike is a wee bit left then there is a clump of trees protecting the end of the clubhouse and a bunker closer to the green. The green has three distinct levels and if you finish on a level above the hole then there is almost no chance of a two putt.

Woking is a little more testing than West Hill or Worplesdon and I would also rate it as just slightly better. It provides for plenty of variety and, in addition, has a quaint but likeable clubhouse – it comes as no surprise that Bernard Darwin was a member for sixty years.

The intriguing 18th at Woking

1895 marked the beginning of **New Zealand** Golf Club, just a few years after Woking, and was designed by Samuel "Mure" Fergusson with later alterations from Tom Simpson. If you want to play in quiet surrounds where most holes are totally private then this can be your golfing refuge.

A more friendly arrival I cannot imagine. As we departed the tiny car park my wife and I were met by the Secretary, Roger Marrett who not only made us feel welcome but entertained us with delightful anecdotes about New Zealand Golf Club and a few of its illustrious past members. There are currently only about 170 members and all of their predecessors are named in gold on the lockers. Numerous lockers featured prefixes such as Colonel and General and, notably, Sir Arthur Conan Doyle.

At only 6000 yards this is not a long course, but believe me, you must be accurate. Every hole features large amounts of heather and the fairways are bordered by a magnificent variety of trees. In front of the trees there is

The 1st hole at New Zealand is one of the few with a wide fairway

often a wall of rhododendrons and occasionally bracken or gorse. On holes such as the longer par 4's on the front nine it is not hard to lose your ball if you are offline. The bunkering at New Zealand is not particularly deep but they are well designed and at times blend imperceptibly into the surrounds. At holes such as 6, 9, 15 and 16 the trees at the sides are wonderfully dense – you could be the only person on the course and you would never know.

The greens were excellent and some, like the eighteenth, had interesting hollows and bumps just short of the green. The modest total length is a reflection of having five par 3's and only one par 5. There are five par 4's that exceed 400 yards (holes 1, 2, 9, 11, and 12) so you don't feel you are playing a short course.

Above: Landing area for the drive is narrow at the par 4, 6th
Below: Approaching the 12th green

I particularly liked the par 4, 2nd and three of the short holes – the third, seventh and sixteenth. Both the tenth and the sixteenth have heather almost all the way to the green. The tenth green has a tiny opening at the front and bunkers covering both sides. You can easily over-club and finish in the shrubs behind the green.

The only par 5 is the 476 yard 14th and although I am not a long hitter I was pin high with my second shot. The par 4, 15th features a ditch on the right edge of the fairway and an interesting V shaped cross-bunker complex just in front of the green. The sixteenth appears a little daunting when you first stand on the tee and observe the forest at the sides and back of the green and a meadow of heather stretching all the way to the greenside bunkers. You would perhaps expect plenty of dog-legs but the only such hole is the par 4, 17th. If you use your driver you are almost certainly going to run out of fairway so position is the key. Pine trees are close to the left as you approach the heavily bunkered green.

Above: Bunkers near the 15th green
Below: The daunting 16th, a par 3 of 200 yards over heather

17th green

Looking back down the 18th at New Zealand

I couldn't imagine anywhere better on a lovely sunny afternoon especially when you are offered a Pimms at the seventh and thirteenth greens.

For our next two heathland courses we headed south, first to **Liphook** and then on to West Sussex. Liphook is just off the A3 to Portsmouth, in Hampshire and directly south of Hankley Common. Turn off at the B2131 and you will see the signs. Liphook is the only course design of Arthur Croome and opened for play as eighteen holes in 1923. Croome's health soon began to fail so it was his partner Tom Simpson who had input in subsequent years although his relationship with the committee could be described as rather strained.

Liphook became a shining example of the move away from penal design philosophies. With Liphook largely in mind, Tom Simpson wrote a letter to The Times: "The promoters of a new course…invariably press for length, because they have been 'got at' by the good player, amateur and professional, the plausible excuse being that, unless the course measure at least 6500 yards, it will be thought nothing of. I confess that when I am asked to lay out a golf course I accept no instructions of matters of this kind, and at all times refuse to lay out a course for the benefit of the tiger."

Simpson had a mound built at the left of the 9th green at Liphook to illustrate his ideas. The 'tiger' line on the right near the heather ridges gives a straight second shot to the green whereas the 'rabbit' will play left to the safe part of the fairway but then has the problem that the hillock is masking his approach.

I don't normally like commencing a round with a par 3 but the first at Liphook is a beauty. With a big hollow between tee and green and a distance of 202 yards, this is no easy start. Birch trees are at both sides of the green which slopes significantly to the right.

Liphook's opening hole

There are quite a few sloping fairways such as the par 4, 2nd where you need to keep your drive to the right but watch for the heather nearby. The par 3, 3rd (139 yards) plays longer as it is up hill and the high heather crested bunkers at the front block out any view of the green. The 4th is a very long par 4 (460 yards) that runs parallel with the second hole. As with most holes at Liphook, there is trouble by way of heather and then trees on both sides. The par 5, 5th is a possible birdie opportunity but keep to the left side as you play to the green.

Playing here for the first time, the par 3, 7th looks like a tricky tee shot even though it measures only 149 yards from the back tee. If you miss the two-tiered green you will either be bunkered or have a difficult recovery shot. The eighth and ninth (see earlier comments) are both pretty holes with valleys, birches and heather.

The eleventh is a difficult short hole featuring a narrow green and three bunkers. One of the holes that I really liked is the short par 5, 13th which is rated Index 8 largely due to the proliferation of heather and the heathery ditch angled across the fairway commencing about 120 yards short of the elevated green.

Above: Approach to the green at the par 5, 13th
Below: The corner of the 16th is an old stone quarry

The run home from here includes a wonderful variety of interesting holes. The 14th is a short par 4 that dog-legs to the right. If you take on too much of the corner you will be in thick heather, bunkers or amongst conifers. This is a great hole but I don't understand why the need for conifers amongst the bunkers and very thick heather. If the conifers were not there then big hitters would be more tempted to try for the green and risk the chance of a heathery grave.

The par 4, 15th is another that bends right but here the dog-leg is in play for the drive which is uphill and over heather. The 16th bends back to the left around an old stone quarry . The drive is downhill but keep away from the left side of the fairway —a lovely quirky hole. At the par 3, 17th you hit uphill over heather so the message is don't be short .

Liphook's 13th hole in Springtime (Photo courtesy Liphhook GC)

The finishing hole is a really good par 5. Although it is only 462 yards, the fairway curves left with heather on both sides. The slope of the terrain will take your ball to the right where there are three bunkers from 80 yards out and another bunker on the left at the green. If the flag is at the front and you finish on the top tier then you will be hard pressed to get anywhere near the hole with your downhill putt. I'm not surprised it is rated Index 6.

The greens were very good and, although the fairways were a little patchy by the end of the summer in 2011, I would ignore this as I was informed by the Secretary, John

The 18th is an excellent finishing hole at Liphhook

Douglass, that a fairway reticulation system was being installed in 2012. Liphook can get rather busy as they have 800 members so I suggest you book your game well in advance. You have to cross what was the old A3 a few times but you still had the feeling of being in the countryside. Liphook was slightly hilly, had plenty of heather and some interesting and somewhat unusual holes which I rather liked.

To the east of Liphook, on the A29 near Pulburough on the way to Littlehampton, in the midst of farming land you will find **West Sussex**. The drive from our B&B at Tilford was longer than I had expected but the traffic was light and the countryside on the borders of the South Downs is very pretty.

There is a genuinely charming and unpretentious atmosphere at West Sussex. My wife and I played early Saturday afternoon and beforehand enjoyed the casual lunch in the dining room with a few of the 'older members'. Give me this over Wentworth any day!

What a great course – it is certainly in my top 5 heathland adventures. There are so many memorable holes, particulary the five par 3's. The heather is profuse from the second hole onwards and the bunkers here are a little larger than on most of the courses we had played to date. The lovely undulating fairways are framed mainly by pines interspersed with birches and oaks.

The opening hole is the only genuine par 5 although the seventh and eleventh are played as a par 5 from the white tees when Stableford or Par competitions are held. The first is pretty straightforward and is one of the few real birdie opportunities. You drive uphill at the second with thick trees and OOB on the left and heather at the right. The ridges across the fairway for your second shot are along the path of an old Roman road.

The par 4, 4th is a lovely dog-leg left with the corner protected by heather and a large bunker. The green is in a pretty setting framed by very tall pines. Back to back par 3's is unusual, but what great holes are the 5th and 6th. The 5th is set amongst the pines whilst the 6th is a long carry (226 yards to the green) over

The very challenging par 3, 6th

a large pond with profuse heather and bracken to the left and bunkers to the right. Short hitters can play it as a par 4 around the right of the pond.

The long par 4, 7th starts with an intimidating uphill drive over a bunker and a large area of heather with pines close to the left. A large oak stands at the very edge of the green on the right hand side and from this side the downhill putt can be rather quick. The 8th is the third par 3 in four holes but they are each completely different. The tee shot here must be dead straight to avoid the bunkers at each side of the front of the green. From the 8th green if you look left there is a great view back down the 16th hole.

The second longest par 3 is the 12th which requires a solid strike of 221 yards. Near the tee is gorse and then heather for much of the hole. Anywhere right is either in the pines or OOB and there are two bunkers at the right of the angled green. The middle of the back nine is extremely picturesque with undulations and plenty of heather. The par 4, 13th also has gorse, broom and a bridle path on the right. The shot into the green needs to be well struck to the raised green with three large bunkers at the front.

We had extra time to admire the views at the 14th tee whilst the horses and their riders strode casually along the bridle track across the fairways. The 14th is one of the standout holes. The downhill drive must be accurate as there are massive amounts of heather as the fairway bends to the right. When playing to the green you have a bunker and gorse on the right and a marshy area with a pond at the left.

The short 15th is played over a small pond with pines and birches enclosing this beautiful setting. The 16th can be a card wrecker. The drive is semi blind up a heather clad hill and then there is a demanding second shot over a deep valley of thick heather and a nasty slope in front of the green.

Top: Par 3, 5th at West Sussex from behind the green
Middle: 8th hole
Above: Par 3, 12th – heather and gorse

The 17th is another long par 4 (440 yards) that turns right. The drive is over heather and bunkers guard the corner of the dog-leg. Don't be fooled by the flat terrain of the final hole – it is harder than it first appears. Apart from all the heather there are four fairway bunkers and another three near the green.

Long par 4, 17th at West Sussex

Whatever you do, you must play West Sussex. If I lived anywhere nearby I would be delighted to be a member – not just for the course but for the lovely ambience here. Interestingly, there are no fairway sprinklers but at the end of summer everything was still quite green. West Sussex is one of Peter Thomson's favourite courses and it is certainly one of mine.

Par 4, 16th from behind

The picturesque 15th at West Sussex

I played the West Course at **Wentworth** on a lovely sunny Friday in late August. The golfing weather gods had smiled on me for a change as the previous day it rained non stop around London and it was one of the few where we had not arranged any golf. Designed by Harry Colt, the West Course opened in 1926 – two years after the East which was also his work. Commencing in 2005, local resident Ernie Els was in charge of reworking the greens and bunkers as well as lengthening several holes. I will comment later on his contentious 18th green.

As you would expect, given the hefty green fees, the course was in immaculate condition. The greens were quite fast but the fairways were a little soft due to the previous days rain and the fact that I imagine they are never allowed to be any colour except a rich green. The bunkers are well designed and maintained and the tree specimens are superb. Whilst there is some heather, to me it felt more parkland rather than heathland.

There are three tees, championship, white and yellow. I will primarily refer to the white tee distances. The first hole is a good opening par 5 with attractive bunkering that gets the field away. The par 3, 2nd looks quite spectacular with its raised green and tiny entrance between two large bunkers. Better to be long with your tee shot and take one extra club as it plays longer than 154 yards.

The 3rd (448 yards) is one of the many very testing par 4's. It plays slightly uphill and has three fairway bunkers on the right to catch your drive and the green is tiered. The par 5, 4th is made more difficult with a tight drive through the trees where the hole bends left to a green with five bunkers close by. At the par 4, 6th they have a novel way of lengthening the hole for tournaments. Behind the white tees is a row of twenty foot tall trees in planter boxes set on rails so that they can be moved aside to open up a tiger tee 67 yards further back.

The 7th is a lovely par 4 requiring an accurate drive through trees. You need to watch for a ditch that runs across the fairway at about the 285 yard mark. The 8th tee invites you to try for length down the hill so as to minimize the danger with the second which must be played over a pond in front of the green. The pond narrows along the left side of the green and a

Above: Wentworth's 1st green on the West Course
Below: Par 3, 2nd hole

large bunker occupies the right hand side. Before heading to the next tee there is the excellent half way hut and hot food awaiting.

Index 1 is the 449 yard par 4, 9th. A duffed drive will find either heather or a ditch beyond which lie two bunkers at the right. Left is a wall of trees and then OOB beside the railway line. A long shot to the green has to negotiate two bunkers blocking much of the front of the green. This is followed by the 10th which is a very pretty par 3 through the pines.

Above: 7th hole
Below: The 9th is rated the hardest hole at Wentworth's West Course

I am a little mystified as to how the par 5, 12th gets the easy Index of number 18. Admittedly it is only 509 yards in length but for starters you have to hit over the top of three pine trees or thread your way through a tiny gap. A ditch comes onto part of the fairway on both sides about half way to the green and then you have to play over a wide burn in front of the green. If that isn't enough, there is OOB at the right for the drive, along the left for your second and behind the green if your third is too strong. Have I missed something here? I suppose the answer is that the 'gorillas' can fly way over the trees and then hit the green in two. I'd like to see how many come unstuck trying that.

The 13th is a very difficult long par 4 that bends left and has a heavily bunkered green. The par 3, 14th (179 yards) plays uphill to a green protected by four bunkers. Anything short will roll back down the steep slope. The 15th is another monster par 4 (477 yards) where you face heather in front of the tee, a wet ditch along the right and a tree that is only marginally left of the middle of the fairway.

The penultimate hole is a lovely looking par 5 of 566 yards that curves left through wall to wall trees on both sides. A wet ditch lies in front of the tee and then there are two fairway bunkers on either side to catch an errant drive.

The only hole I disliked was the par 5, 18th. The hole makes a big dog-leg to the right so it is crucial that you leave your second in good position for the difficult shot into the green. A very wide burn runs on an angle from the left at the front of the

Top: Par 3, 10th
Middle: Pine trees block your drive at the 12th
Bottom: The 15th is another tight driving hole

slightly raised green that is ridiculously narrow in depth and has three bunkers at the back. The green slopes to the front and is only a few feet beyond the burn which is considerably wider at this point so spinning your ball back into the water is a real possibility. Sorry Ernie, but this green spoils the round for me.

Even from the most forward (yellow) tees the West is a very healthy 6731 yards. It is a very good course and has the added allure that comes from seeing big tournaments played there. These include the 1953 Ryder Cup and the World Matchplay which was held at Wentworth from 1964 till 2007.

Par 5, 17th

There is a handicap limit of 18 for both men and women if you want to play the West but, on the day of my visit, there seemed to be some males on the course that were not in that category. The atmosphere in the clubhouse where I ate with a member was more one of money and business people. I rarely ever mention green fees but I will in this one instance. Wentworth did not even reply to my emails requesting a game in preparation for this book so I organized to play with a member at a cost of 95 pounds, being a Friday in summer. The unaccompanied visitors fee is a massive 360 pounds which includes the compulsory use of a caddy. Even in mid winter the fee is 195 pounds so you had better pray for good weather.

I had not heard much of **The Addington** but I was partly influenced in booking a game due to the nostalgic regard that P G Wodehouse held for it. Located just south of Croydon, it is hilly, quirky and has beautiful trees, all of which would convince you that this is in the heart of the countryside. However when you play the fourteenth and see the London skyline you realise that you are just thirteen miles from the City.

Not only did J F Abercromby design The Addington (in 1912) but he founded the club and ran it for the first twenty years as a 'benevolent dictator'. Upon hearing a visitor enquire as to the location of the suggestion box, he once responded "I am the suggestion box." Originally there were two courses built but the one known as the New Course was lost to housing development just after the Second World War. Had he still been alive, one could imagine 'Aber' standing in front of the bulldozers to protect this destruction.

It had rained for the two previous days so the first few holes, which are more parkland than heathland, were a little wet under foot. The 1st and 3rd are uphill par 3's, the 2nd is a long par 5 and holes four and five are each long par 4's of 437 yards. At this stage I was feeling somewhat underwhelmed by the experience but I remembered one of the members telling me that it all happens from the sixth. How right he was!

The par 4, 6th dog-legs sharply to the left where you then play to a green bordered by a huge crater on the right and the deepest bunker I have ever seen. P G Wodehouse famously used to give his address as:

> c/o the sixth bunker
>
> The Addington
>
> Croydon, Surrey.

Above: The 'Wodehouse' bunker at the 6th
Below: Par 3, 7th at The Addington

I recall cautioning my wife to avoid this bunker at all costs as she could be there for the day. She unfortunately got to take the fifteen or so steps just to get into the bunker and to my amazement got out in one and holed the putt.

The soil from here onwards seemed to have more sand and gravel and most holes now had plenty of heather. The par 3, 7th is a lovely short hole with the green set into the side of a heather clad hill. Keep a little left to avoid bunkers and some nasty lies in the heather on the right.

There are some deep chasms at The Addington but they have made the course rather more easy walking by the use of long raised footbridges. The par 4, 9th is as quirky as it gets. The tee shot is over a very deep heather and bracken filled hollow to a plateau where you then play

Top: *The first of the chasms at the 9th*
Middle: *11th hole*
Bottom: *Looking back from the 12th green*

over another deep hollow to the green. It is an easy hole if you hit two solid strikes but you could score a big number especially if you end up in the first hollow.

The 11th is a very short par 3 of only 136 yards, but with plenty of bunkers and heather you need to hit the green with your tee shot. The par 5, 12th is just 486 yards but is rated Index 4. Not having played here before was a big disadvantage as this is a hole where it is brains, not brawn, that will win the day. The drive is over a hill where the fairway bends left down a steep bumpy slope covered in light rough and heather and then the green is high up on a hill. The safe approach is to hit your tee shot only about 200 yards to the top of the first hill. If you go for the drive then you take pot luck as to where your ball will end up on the down slope.

The 13th is a magnificent long par 3 of 229 yards played through a narrow clearing on the side of a hill. I would love to see this hole in spring when the rhododendrons and other shrubs are in bloom. Henry Longhurst went so far as to say that it is "with the exception of the 5th at Pine Valley, Philadelphia, the greatest one shot hole in inland golf."

The par 4, 14th plays downhill and provides views of the distant London skyline. The 15th is one of the more difficult par 4's at 433 yards and uphill. The next two holes are exhilarating tests of golf. At the par 5, 16th we were accompanied by an inquisitive fox. You must keep to the middle of the fairway for the dangerous shot into the green perched above a ravine that lies to the front and right. The 17th is a difficult par 3 where you play over the

Above: The brilliant par 3, 13th at The Addington
Below: Par 3, 17th from above the 16th green

same ravine to a green surrounded by trouble. To the right you are either bunkered or in heather but to the left is probably a lost ball in thick trees.

The final hole seems to revert back to the parkland feel of the first five holes. The greens looked as though they could be quite tricky if they were fast but they had been scarified only a week or so before our game. The fairways were acceptable but do not have a reticulation system. The Addington is definitely worth playing just for some of the unusual holes. You could feel that this was once a top course so I thought it appropriate when a member told me that the course was improving again "after twenty years of neglect."

I had been told that **Swinley Forest** was a 'must play' with the proviso that first you have to find a way to get on the course. Many of the private clubs are access only through high gates and secured perimeters so you can't just drive in, look at a few holes and take some photographs. I sent several emails which went unanswered so Michael Hughes, a friend of mine from Commonwealth Golf Club who lives part of the year in Bray near Ascot, kindly drove to Swinley to explain my situation and, hopefully, arrange a tee time. I won't go into all the details but let's just say that the Secretary's demeanor towards me was rather frosty (this was in August 2011 and I believe a new Secretary is now at Swinley). At this stage it was late morning and raining heavily but I figured I would probably never get another chance to experience Swinley Forest so we ventured into the gloom with just one other pair looking like they would leave the otherwise deserted bar.

The first is a good looking opening hole played over a valley and uphill to a green

Above: 1st and 18th at Swinley Forest, just before the storm
Below: Even in pouring rain the 3rd hole is 'pretty as a picture'

flanked by heather and beautiful Scots Pines which are a feature here. The 2nd is a short par 4 (367 yards) that is surprisingly rated Index 5. The uphill drive over heather is semi blind and from there it is downhill to the green. At this point the rain was getting heavier. I don't mind playing in rain but it frustrates my attempts to get good photos so my wife and I sheltered under umbrellas and called the two behind us through, knowing there was no-one else to follow. Standing behind the second green the view down the short par 4, 3rd was so picturesque I decided to take some photos from under my umbrella in the heavy rain.

The short holes at Swinley Forest are all very good, none better than the 184 yard 4th which Harry Colt went on to attempt to replicate elsewhere. There is heather most of the way to the green set into the side of the hill.

The 4th hole as viewed in Spring and Autumn

Left: 4th (Photo courtesy Ben Jarvis)
Below: Colt's stunning 4th hole

The 5th is the only par 5 at Swinley Forest

12th hole

Anything straight but short will roll back so there is really no place to be other than on the green. Perhaps it was just my perception but three of the short holes, the 4th, 10th and 13th all looked longer than their yardage.

Swinley measures just 6000 yards even from the back tees and there is only one par 5, the 5th, but there are six par 4's of over 400 yards. The 5th has a heathery ridge beside a drain on the right that runs into a lily pond where the fairway dog-legs to the right. If you block your drive you may finish in the rhododendrons that are before the pond. Although you can't see it, a racecourse runs along the left side of the sixth and seventh. The par 4, 7th climbs uphill to a green from where there are lovely views across parts of the course. After the short 8th with its raised green that is built up on three sides you then encounter the third par 4 in four holes that is over 400 yards.

The 13th is another great short hole

The 13th in Springtime (Photo courtesy Ben Jarvis)

Long Par 4, 15th

18th and clubhouse at Swinley Forest

Par 3, 17th

The long par 4, 12th (455 yards) requires a good drive over heather with two bunkers at the right. Two more bunkers cross much of the fairway about fifty yards out from the green. The par 3, 13th features lots of heather and reminded me of the 16th at New Zealand. Every hole is pretty at Swinley Forest but none more so than the green setting at the 15th where you play uphill for your second shot.

At the par 3, 17th do not make my mistake and go through the back of the green where your ball will run down a steep bank into undergrowth from which you will have little hope of making an easy recovery. The 18th is a short par 4 that plays initially downhill towards a ditch beyond which there are several fairway bunkers you need to avoid on the upslope toward the green.

This is a really beautiful course in a very quiet secluded setting. The terrain is hilly without being too steep, the trees are magnificent and although there is plenty of heather there are not too many long carries. The greens had some interesting undulations but were rather slow and with all the rain the whole course was quite soft.

On a sunny day this would be just about the best place to be playing golf. Swinley dates back to 1909 and I rather fancy that Harry Colt was being overly modest when he described it as his 'least bad course'. It can be hard to find and is located south of The Berkshire and west of Sunningdale just off the A322.

If you are departing the UK via Gatwick then **Walton Heath** can be your finale round. It is located just north of the airport on the B2032, past Junction 8 on the M25. The **Old Course** was designed by Herbert Fowler who was the brother in law of the club's founder, Sir Cosmo Bonsor. It opened for play in 1904 and for the next 46 years the great James Braid served as their first professional.

Most club histories are pretty dull affairs, a notable exception being Phil Pilley's account of Walton Heath's first 100 years. In it he quotes from Horace Hutchinson and a 1904 edition of Country Life: "The heath is a delightful place, only sixteen miles from London and nearly 700 feet high. It is covered with heather and gorse, and if there are no grouse and black game there ought to be. There are rabbits and partridges, and now there are also golfers." [1].

Walton Heath can boast many great events and achievements with four prime Ministers as members as well as a reigning monarch. In 1935 the Duke of Windsor was Club Captain and later that year he became King Edward VIII.

I can't think of any other course where the length of so many holes varies by such a large distance in comparing the 'daily' tees with the back tees. In totality you are comparing 6361 yards with a frighteningly long 7462 yards.

The start is unusual in that it is a par 3 and is the only hole on the same side of the busy road as the clubhouse. Before going any further I should stress that both courses at Walton Heath have more heather

[1]*"Heather and Heaven – Walton Heath Golf Club 1903–2003" Phil Pilley*

than any other near London and there is no hole where it is not an ever present hazard. I will refer to 'daily' tee yardages and occasionally the back tees in brackets. The par 4, 3rd is the first of many very long two shot holes at 451 yards with trees left and heather right. At the 4th you face a par 4 of 441 yards that blows out to a massive 519 from the back. Three bunkers are in play for your long second shot.

The fifth is a lovely hole that sweeps left as it plays slightly downhill. Apart from all the heather, the danger is a bunker left of center about 43 yards out and then one each side of the green. One of the best short holes is the 189 yard (222) 11th which has very thick rough for anything short and four greenside bunkers. Danger lurks at the par 4, 12th which has a big dog-leg to the right and with broken ground approximately 50 yards before the green. Two par 5's follow and at the fourteenth in particular there are very large amounts of heather, especially around the bunkers.

Above: 5th hole of the Old Course, Walton Heath
Below: Plenty of heather as you approach the 14th green

The sixteenth will stay in your memory. This is a terrific hole which turns left and with bunkers along the right hand side. The fairway narrows about 150 yards out as you play uphill to a raised green with a heathery mound left and a deep bunker right. From the front tees this hole is a par 5 of 535 yards but for tournaments it becomes a challenging par 4 of 475 yards. When I first played the Old Course back in 1998 the 17th, a lovely par 3 of 181 yards, was an island green with a semi-circle bunker at the front. I noticed in 2011 that the middle section has been filled in leaving one bunker either side.

The 18th is a substantial par 4 of 404 (479) yards. The tee shot is uphill with two bunkers at the left for the drive and then you face a trademark Herbert Fowler cross bunker which covers the whole width of the fairway. If you take too much club to clear the bunker and you are through the green then OOB is not far away. When referring to the cross bunker at the eighteenth, Bernard Darwin said: "There is no way round; we must harden our hearts and play the shot." He concluded "there is no

Par 3, 17th Old Course, with the new bunker arrangement

monotony of high pitching but plenty of running up to be done and the fast, firm turf is exactly suited to the purpose. That is another thing which heightens the delightful illusion that we are playing seaside golf. In short, if there is anything that golfers want and do not get at Walton Heath, I do not know what it can be."

The **New Course** at Walton Heath, also designed by Fowler, commenced as nine holes in 1907 and six years later the full eighteen holes were completed. Many of the holes run alongside those of the Old so, as you would expect, both courses are very

2nd hole of the New Course

Par 3, 6th from behind the green, New Course

Looking towards the 5th green, New Course

similar. The New is slightly shorter and has no weaknesses but it could be said has no real stand out holes. Probably the best are the fifth, fourteenth and eighteenth.

The round starts with a short par 4 and a not too difficult par 3. The 3rd is more typical of the Old Course being a par 4 of 419 yards where the fairway narrows about 250 yards from the tee. The lovely 5th (Index 1) is a lengthy two shot hole of 461 yards that runs downhill and dog-legs right at about 210 yards from the tee. The par 3, 6th has clumps of heather short of the green and two small bunkers at the front right.

At the 7th you need to avoid the cross bunker 47 yards from the green whilst the par 5, 8th bends left with heather and broken ground 270 yards from the tee and thick trees all along the right. The par 4, 9th features similar hazards to the previous hole. The fourteenth requires two very precise shots as it is almost a double dog-leg with the fairway narrowing near the green and plenty of heather on both sides. At the par 5, 16th (511 yards front tee and 607 back tee) the fairway runs out for about 30 yards at 313 yards from the tee.

Above: Bunkers at the 11th
Below: Par 4, 13th at the New Course, Walton Heath

The par 4, 17th plays downhill with a gorse-clad gully in front of the green. In many ways the final hole is similar to the eighteenth on the Old Course. You play over the same gully in front of the tee and then have to negotiate a large cross- bunker in front of the long green. Another bunker lies at the back left for the long pulled second shot.

During the round we were fortunate to have the company of Ken Macpherson who had not long retired after over thirty years as just the third club professional at Walton Heath. Ken is a delightful man and showed us the wonderful memorabilia of James Braid and Harry Busson, the latter being a renowned club maker as well as the club's second professional. Despite Ken's wise advice I have to admit that the New

Course got the better of me. A steady crosswind blew all day and, as Ken commented, this well and truly brings the heather into play.

The fairways and greens here are first class – the British Senior Open had been played on the Old Course only a week or so earlier. The clubhouse and meals were excellent and the practice putting green rivals Little Aston's as one of the best in Britain.

Ken Macpherson insisted that we visit an unusual little course nearby by the name of **Reigate Heath**. It is easy to find just south of Walton Heath and is only a very short distance from Reigate Town. This is a genuine little gem with lovely views over valleys to neighbouring hills and has the unusual feature of a large old windmill right behind the clubhouse.

Reigate Heath began right back in 1895 after Lady Somerset provided the land and Tom Dunn laid out nine holes. She imposed the condition that lady members should have equal rights in every way- and this was twenty six years before they had the vote in Britain.

It might be only 5658 yards but this is a wonderful little course that is a lot of fun. On a number of the holes the alternate tees are quite different so you don't feel like you are playing the same nine holes twice. You may play over the green you have just left and a few minor roads run across the course but it all somehow works without too many problems.

On my first visit I stood on what I thought was the first tee high up where you hit across a steep bank of gorse and heather and play a short approach to the elevated green. However, that was the tenth (alternate) tee. The first tee is hidden away below the clubhouse and requires a different line to the green.

At the par 4, 2nd you drive over the first green whereas when playing it as the 11th you are to the side of the green and the drive is straight ahead. At about 95 yards short of the green the fairway stops and there is 30 yards of heather before the apron. The 3rd is a great par 3 uphill that is 183 yards but stretches to a much tougher 220 yards as the 12th. Five bunkers guard this green.

When you play the 484 yard 4th it is a par 5 but as the 13th it is a par 4 of 447 yards, making it Index 1. At the 300 yard area the fairway makes a 90 degree left turn. The 5th and 14th are similar in length and require a drive over heather onto a narrow fairway through the trees. The par 3, 6th is 226 yards over a slight hollow covered with heather. One bunker lies at either side of the green where the distance is shortened to 186 yards when played as the 15th.

The opening green as played from the 10th tee

Par 3, 9th/18th, clubhouse and windmill

The 7th is a short uphill par 4 of 307 yards. You have to hit over the sixth green and a local road to the split-level green which has a bunker either side and a deeper one at the very front. The sixteenth tee is at the right of the previous green and brings into play a large oak tree on the right. The eighth and seventeenth play as much the same for this short par 4 that runs uphill to a green with two bunkers. The entrance road to the golf club runs all along the right of the fairway.

One of the prettiest is the short finishing hole with the windmill as a backdrop. It runs slightly uphill over heathery mounds and there are four bunkers dotted around the green. It is rated the easiest hole as the 136 yard 9th but becomes Index 13 as the 156 yard 18th.

There are 600 members here in this very family orientated club. The clubhouse was recently refurbished and the meals are excellent. Reigate Heath is well worth a visit.

Looking towards the 2nd/11th green from the 10th tee

SOUTH WEST ENGLAND

After departing the joys of Surrey, the journey is west to Dorset, Devon and finally Cornwall. First stop is at **Ferndown** Golf Club on the A31, 6 miles north of Bournemouth.

Ferndown was founded in 1913 and a year later the course was opened. Designer was Harold Hilton, a distinguished amateur golfer who won two Open Championships. Located on ideal sandy soil, Ferndown is noted for its conditioning. It was here that Percy Allis was the professional for over twenty five years.

Pine and heather go hand in hand at Ferndown. The number of dog-legs makes keeping on the fairways crucial. In spring when the rhododendrons are flowering the course takes on an 'Augusta' appearance. Bunkers are rather plentiful with many having fairly steep lips. The course is not super long at around 6500 yards from the back tees but has hosted some important events such as the 1989 Women's British Open.

You know what to expect after you have played the opening hole, a par 4 of 396 yards. Pines run along both sides and there is one fairway bunker at the left for your drive. This is no easy start as there are then six more bunkers commencing at around 70 yards out from the green.

The 3rd and 4th are both fairly long par 4's, each very well bunkered. The par 3, 5th is 206 yards and has its share of hazards. The tee shot needs to clear a stream and then there are four bunkers in front of the green. Another difficult hole follows at the 6th which measures 409 yards and is rated the hardest hole at Ferndown. The second shot plays uphill where there is a cluster of bunkers beginning at about 100 yards out from the green plus another two greenside.

The three par 5's, the 7th, 10th and 13th , are all genuine dog-legs as are the long par 4's at the 9th,11th15th and 18th. In a nutshell, you need to be able to work the ball both ways to have any chance of a good score.

I'm not sure whether they really want visitors at Ferndown. They once tried to charge Tom Doak a green fee just to walk around the course and I have heard many comments from visitors that members just played through and treated them rather disdainfully. As for my own experience – they refuse to answer my emails and when a friend of mine in Scotland rang them on my behalf they did not bother to return his call!

There are three other good heathland layouts in close proximity just a little to the south, namely Broadstone, Parkstone and Isle of Purbeck.

Broadstone is just a few miles north of Poole –from the A31 take the A349 for a short distance and then the B3074. Set in a lovely estate of 250 acres, the original 1898 design was by Tom Dunn. In 1914 much of the course was redesigned by Harry Colt who routed holes 5 –16 out of parkland and into heathland terrain. The new course re-opened in 1920 and then had some later input from Herbert Fowler.

The course is gently undulating and has many greens in lovely settings amongst pine trees. Heather, gorse and rhododendrons add to the extent that Bernard Darwin once labelled Broadstone as the 'Gleneagles of the south.' The back nine offers some lovely views of the surrounding countryside and Poole Harbour.

Above: Approaching the 7th green at Broadstone
Below: Don't be short at the par 3, 8th
(Photos courtesy David Morgan / Broadstone GC)

You need to be well prepared from the start as the par 5, 1st hole has a stream along the right and it then crosses the fairway at the dog-leg. There is plenty of heather all along the right before you reach the green set in front of the pines. The 3rd is a fairly short downhill par 4 but you need to play over a pond well in front of the green. There is also a pond at the right of the fourth green but it is only in play for a poor shot. The 5th is a short par 4 initially uphill and then downhill over a large cross-bunker. I can't help wondering whether our friend Mr Fowler left his calling card here.

The par 4, 7th (422 yards) will test you with a very tricky shot to the green where you must first play over a deep gully with a lengthy cross bunker amongst the heather. This is followed by a long par 3 of 203 yards where you once more play over a heather filled gully. There is one bunker short left and three to the right of the green – in brief, don't be short.

The par 4, 10th is a very tight drive to a fairway that slopes to the right. There is thick heather and bracken along the left whilst the right has three fairway and one greenside bunker. Anything further right is in a line of trees. The twelfth is uphill and bends right and heather prevails on both sides.

One of the best and most difficult holes is the 13th, a par 4 of 442 yards. The fairway angles left near the green so you need to keep your drive to the right. The green is set into the side of the hill and has some

Above: 13th from side on
Below: Short par 4, 14th (Photo courtesy David Morgan / Broadstone GC)

deep bunkers on the lower left side. Like the other shorter par 4's, the 14th requires you to carry bunkers for your uphill second shot.

The short 15th (196 yards) plays from a raised tee. You need to avoid two bunkers short of the green and another two that are greenside. I love the look of the approach to the greens on Harry Colt's par 3's (eg. Sunningdale and Swinley Forest), and this is no exception.

Two precise shots are needed at the par 4, 17th. Trees jut out to the edge of the fairway on the right and then a burn is in play for a weak second hit. The enjoyable round concludes with a par 4 that dog-legs left around trees to a green with some interesting bunker placements.

Broadstone should definitely be on your itinerary if you are anywhere near Dorset – I'm sure it would be better known if it was closer to the heathland belt around Surrey.

Parkstone is just east of Poole near the A338. Initially the course was the work of Willie Park Jnr in 1909 but the current course dates back to around 1937 after the revisions by James Braid. In 1996 the course was designated as a SSSI site which proved to be a blessing in disguise as it enabled the club to remove thousands of pines which were encroaching on the native grasses. Following on from his father at nearby Ferndown, Peter Allis was the professional at Parkstone from 1957–1970.

The par 4, 1st requires an interesting second shot into the green where there is a high treed bank at the left and three bunkers to the right. The tee at the short second is amongst trees and the green is dominated by the high grassy bank at the rear. The short par 5 , 3rd is a lovely hole that starts out beside a pond. The drive is over heather and is followed by a blind second over a hill and then to a sloping green with a hedge at the back. I love tricky short par 4's such as the fourth. It is only 282 yards but the landing area for most drives features heathery ridges running vertically along the fairway. The short approach is toughened up with two bunkers short of the green and another four further on. Despite its modest length it is rated the eleventh hardest.

The 7th is a delightful par 3 of 173 yards that plays uphill over thick rough. There are five greenside bunkers and pine trees to the right. There are no bunkers at the par 5, 8th which runs uphill all the way to an elevated and hidden green.

The twelfth is another good short two shot hole that dog-legs left with heather and one deep bunker near the green. There aren't too many flat holes at Parkstone. The short fourteenth is downhill over grassy mounds and then four bunkers protect the green. The 15th is a difficult par 4 of 422 yards that bends left. You need to watch for pines on the left and rough along the right.

The par 3, 16th is a pretty hole, downhill over heather banks and with three bunkers at the front and right of the target. The penultimate hole is a long three shotter that turns right and plays uphill to a raised green. The challenge is definitely not over until you have completed the 201 yard par 3, 18th. The green is higher up and is angled to the left with one bunker either side.

Parkstone has some hilly terrain and is a good seaside heathland course with a modest length of 6241 yards. The golfing experience is enhanced by views over Poole Harbour to Brownsea Island and the coastal downs of the Isle of Purbeck.

South of Poole on the A351 for a few miles and then the B3351 will take you to Isle of Purbeck Golf Club which dates back to 1892. Harry Colt was involved in course modifications in 1925.

Isle of Purbeck is worth playing just for the magnificent coastal views and the fabulous fifth hole. There are only a few stands of pines so this is almost links golf with lots of heather and gorse if you can't stay on the short grass. It is only a little over 6200 yards from the back tees but the hills and the wind can make a mockery of yardage.

The 371 yard par 4, 1st may seem like a gentle start but you must not go through the back of the green where a steep bank will make recovery difficult. The 2nd is 417 yards and features a burn and then a number of bunkers near the green.

The fifth tee is set high up in this protected heathland wilderness. The views of Poole Harbour and across to the Solent are just superb. The 404 yard 5th snakes downhill towards the sea with the fairway becoming very narrow as it falls away on both sides where there are plenty of bunkers in amongst the heather. This is followed by a short par 5 that is rated Index 1 partly because it plays longer being uphill all the way.

The 194 yard par 3, 11th (The Island) is a potential card wrecker if you play a poor tee shot. You play downhill over a valley thick with heather. There are large bunkers on both sides of the front of the green and pine trees further to the side. From the 10th and 12th tees you can't help but notice the massive amounts of heather on this part of the course.

I have yet to see a course with involvement from Harry Colt that has had weak short holes. The par 3, 15th (Crater) will also test you with heather if you are short, gorse if you are long or wide and four greenside bunkers.

Isle of Purbeck is definitely worth a game but I would try for a day that is not too windy. Dorset is not often thought of as a golfing destination but with these four courses in close proximity it's not a bad place to spend a week of your golfing holiday.

Heading west along the A35 and then the coastal road to Budleigh Salterton brings us to the delightful heathland layout of **East Devon** Golf club which pretty much lies along the cliff-top above the town. To say that the scenery here is spectacular is something of an understatement, especially around the fifteenth and sixteenth holes with views to Otter Head and along the World Heritage Jurassic Coast – but try for a day when the sea mist doesn't come rolling in.

The round commences with a lovely looking par 4 of 346 yards. The fairway slopes to the right where there are trees and then OOB. The left is particularly heavy with heather. The second is of similar length and runs parallel, returning to the clubhouse. Heather is at both sides and the green has some tricky slopes.

The 411 yard 3rd is uphill, dog-legs slightly to the right and is rated the hardest hole at East Devon. The gradual climb uphill continues at the par 3, 4th and par 4, 5th. The 6th is the first of two par 5's. You need to watch for rough on the left about 50 yards out and a greenside bunker at the right. Don't run through the back of this green.

The 7th is a good par 4 that runs uphill and bends left. The fairway is lined with trees and gorse and slopes to the right so a slight draw is the ideal tee shot. Another good hole follows at the 206 yard 8th which continues uphill. The long par 3 is made more difficult by bunkers at the front on both sides of the green and mounds along the right.

Whilst the 468 yard 9th appears to be a long two shot hole, it is downhill all the way to the green set into the side of a bank at the left. The par 3, 10th is 148 yards but a new tee will add a further 16 yards. This is another uphill short hole with bunkers both sides and a large one in front of the three tiered green. The 12th is the last of the par 5's. The fairway runs uphill and dog-legs right and has gorse and trees for any wayward shots. Your approach to the green can be blocked by two bunkers at the right and a tree on the left.

The short par 4, 15th (304 yards) rises to higher ground where the views are superb. You need to keep your drive to the left to avoid a large fairway bunker. 'Otter View', the par 4, 16th , looks across the beach to the mouth of the River Otter and beyond. As of September 2012 this hole has been slightly changed due to coastal erosion problems. The right hand side of the old fairway will become a public walkway and is OOB. This now gives the hole a slight bend from left to right.

The seventeenth will polarize opinions and can ruin your card. It is a very tough par 4 of 453 yards featuring a deep valley with heather if you are short and gorse at the sides. Another hollow, this time grassed, is hard to see and lies just in front of the green. Cliff-top erosion will require this tee to be moved slightly inland but the views will not be lost.

The 18th is an attractive short par 4 that bends right. There is plenty of heather and some gorse along the right side of the fairway where there is also one bunker for a long drive. The green has two bunkers to the front and grassy banks and hummocks back and right.

East Devon is an enjoyable 6200 yards of heathland with great views from the cliffs 400 feet above the sea. The course has been in existence since 1902 with the enchanting layout benefitting from the influences of Herbert Fowler and Harry Colt. You should definitely add East Devon to your play list.

The A38 is a little inland and will take you along the edge of the Dartmoor Forest to Plymouth in Cornwall, the last location for this journey. Just beyond Plymouth where you cross the Tamar River at Saltash there is a sign to **China Fleet** Country Club. Several golf professionals

Top: East Devon's 15th green from behind
Above: Looking across the 16th green to Otter Head
(Photos courtesy East Devon GC)

China Fleet and the Tamar River (Photo courtesy China Fleet Country Club)

in the Cornwall area had recommended a game at China Fleet. The name seemed so out of character with all the other courses in this locality we felt compelled to at least check it out and see for ourselves exactly what was China Fleet Country Club.

The name comes from the fact that the Country Club was developed from the proceeds of the sale of the Royal British Navy's China Fleet Club in Hong Kong. The Club was opened in 1991 and is situated in 180 acres of lovely Cornish countryside on the banks of the Tamar River. The course design was by Martin Hawtree.

An interesting feature of China Fleet is the use that has been made of the original stone walls on the farmland site. Many of the walls have been partially kept so that they run at angles across the fairways to make tee shots tighter and provide a hazard for anything offline. Whilst the course is not long from the yellow tees (6254 yards), from the back (white) tees it is a reasonable test at 6551 yards.

The par 4, 1st hole is 401 yards and runs down to a green with picturesque views over the Tamar River below. The signature hole here is undoubtedly the 170 yard par 3, 5th. The line to the green is made very narrow by the presence of large trees on both sides. A deep gully and stream must also be negotiated and will be the resting place of either a duffed tee shot or anything that clips the edges of the intruding trees.

As you walk off the green of the par 3, 15th if you have avoided the stone walls then you might be heading for a good score but first you have to get past the tricky sixteenth and seventeenth holes. The par 4, 16th is something of a make-or-break hole where you have to decide whether you are going to hit across the

Above: Narrow par 3, 5th from behind the green
Below: China Fleet
(Photos courtesy China Fleet Country Club)

edge of the water hazard and, if so, care needs to be taken so as not to push your ball too far right as the angled fairway will deflect you into trees or a ditch that runs along this side. Any ball not on the fairway will result in a very difficult shot to the elevated green.

There are three very long two shot holes – the 4th (467 yards), 11th (442 yards) and 17th which is 464 yards and is rated Index number 2. The par 5, 18th is a good finishing hole but at only 511 yards in length is a birdie opportunity.

China Fleet was in good condition when we played and was an enjoyable walk in a pretty setting.

A few miles to the north via the A388 is the resort of **St Mellion**. It is an easy drive, but you can be forgiven if you miss the village which, when I was last there, consisted of one tiny store and an old church. The complex at St Mellion occupies 450 acres in the beautiful Tamar Valley and was originally built by the Bond Brothers. It consists of two eighteen hole courses, a short nine hole layout and both hotel and cottage accommodation. We found the golf villas to be excellent accommodation and are mainly situated not far from the 18th hole of the **Kernow Course**.

In 2008 twenty million pounds was spent upgrading the resort and building nine new holes on what was formerly known as the Old Course. It was originally built in the mid 1970's and in 1979 hosted the Benson & Hedges International. After the recent redevelopment the Old Course was renamed as the Kernow Course.

The opening par 5 is a combination of the old first and second holes. Holes 2 – 5 are from the old layout but some new bunkering has been added. Holes 6 – 12 are all new with the sixth featuring an approach over a hedge to the green. The 10th is a tricky risk and reward type of par 4 and holes eleven and twelve have great views overlooking the Nicklaus Course –as did the old second and third holes. At the short fourteenth club selection can be quite difficult. The narrow green is well below the tee and is located just beyond a pond with steep banks. The temptation is to take too much club which can leave you with a nasty hanging lie above the green and with your next shot chipping back towards the water.

The 15th is a delightful short dog-leg par 5 of 476 yards. The tee shot is over a pond close by and is up a steep hill. You need to keep left to shorten the hole, but this brings in to play a fairway bunker or long grass and water if you are too far left. The second shot may need to be a lay-up followed by a chip hard left of the fairway and over a narrow burn. The green setting is a gem: a stone cottage at the back, running water at the front and often a gathering of ducks watching from under the trees close by.

The 16th is a long par 3 of 227 yards, well bunkered and trouble if you go through the green. The par 4, 17th is a new hole that requires that you land your drive on one of the two plateaus for your shot to the green. The 18th was a tough dog-leg par 4 where your drive had to negotiate a large tree in the middle of the fairway around 210 yards from the tee. Now the hole still has a demanding tee shot but returns back to the clubhouse.

The premier layout is the **Nicklaus Course** which opened in 1986 and was the first Jack Nicklaus design in the UK. Major professional events have been held here nearly every year since 1988. The course plays much longer than its 6651 yards and I must say that I was rather tired after walking and playing here.

Some of the early holes run down a valley with a creek and large mature trees on the left and rather expensive looking homes along the right. The par 4, 3rd is a good two shotter requiring a precise drive and the short par 4, 5th is pretty as a picture. Water comes into play on holes ten, eleven and twelve.

The signature hole, and by far the most attractive, is the lovely par 3, 11th where you play from an elevated tee over a pond to a green in an amphitheatre setting. Trees are close by, especially on the right, and there are two greenside bunkers. The hill behind the green is a great viewing point during tournaments.

The par 5, 12th can certainly cause problems. The downhill fairway is quite narrow with a thick line of large pines all the way down the left. The right hand side slopes away to a fast running creek below fairway level and which eventually comes across the fairway in front of the green.

Index 1 is the fifteenth which is a slight dog-leg right and plays uphill. The narrow fairway is littered with small mounds that were so obviously not made by Mother Nature that I personally would rate it as embarrassing if I were a golf course architect. The last four holes all play long with none tougher than the 18th, a par 4 of 460 yards. Not only is the hole long but it dog-legs to the right. The shot into the green

Par 3, 11th Nicklaus Course, St Mellion (Photo courtesy St Mellion International Resort)

14th at the Nicklaus Course (Photo courtesy St Mellion International Resort)

is made more difficult due to a pond at the left edge and some moguls and deep bunkers on the right.

The Nicklaus Course is not suited to beginners and, whilst I hate carts, you may need one here as the back nine can be heavy going. When I first played at St Mellion in 1996 I preferred the enjoyment factor of what was then the Old Course. On a second visit two years later, again in mid summer, the Nicklaus Course which is on lower ground, was completely under water and the Old Course bunkers were deep with water to the extent that being in any of them meant lost ball. That's the English summer for you.

Near St Mellion is the National Trust rated Cotehele. This fortified house has been owned by the Edgcumbe family for 600 years. The gardens on the hillside face the sun and are protected from the wind and as a result this little area has its own microclimate. As you stroll down to the Tamar River below, you can see a large Roman aqueduct. The shrubs and trees are almost sub-tropical. Several restored old sailing ships are moored nearby at the Cotehele Quay where time has stood still for the last one hundred and fifty years.

Heading further west there are two other non links courses you may come across, namely Looe and Lanhydrock. Near the very pretty town of Looe is the golf club by the same name. I mainly went there because the original layout of the 1930's was by Harry Vardon. Parts of the course are quite high providing excellent views but I couldn't see anything to really recommend a game here. The opening hole is rather intriguing being an unusual par 3. A large tree lies in the middle of the fairway so the only approach is a lofted shot which must clear both the tree on the fairway and miss a number of other trees on the left and at the back of the green. I wonder how many try to chance a bunt along the ground –not really how you want to begin your round.

Lanhydrock Golf Club is inland to the north west near the town of Bodmin. This is a relatively new course (I'm guessing it is about twenty five years old) with water in play on a number of holes. Whilst the greens were good, this is a typical parkland course that can get wet under foot pretty quickly. I recall the par 4, 14th as being a challenging hole where anything left is lost ball or OOB. As with Looe, I can't really recommend this layout as being anything special.

On the A390 near the town of St Austell is **Carlyon Bay** Golf Club. The course is owned by the Brend Hotel Group, but the original owners of the splendid hotel were the Carlyon Family, hence the name of the course.

Whilst Carlyon Bay golf course runs along the coastal cliffs, the fairways are very much parkland. With the first nine holes overlooking St Austell Bay this is a very scenic setting. Although the first two holes are not particularly difficult, the fairway literally runs to the edge of a cliff and then has a drop of several hundred feet to the beach below. On a really windy day I'm sure many balls must disappear down the cliff face.

Not only does OOB on the right towards the sea come into play on many of the first nine holes, but the 9th, 'Quarry', has two additional hazards. The fairway slopes to the right towards the cliff edge and there is a line of four bunkers in play on the left side. Forget about taking the shortcut slightly left of the bunkers down the neighbouring fairway as the white stakes mark that this is also OOB. The 9th is only 350 yards and for the average male golfer is probably just a good drive and a 7 iron, but for many lady

Carlyon Bay as seen from the 1st fairway with St Austell Bay on the right (Photo courtesy Brend Hotels)

golfers there is a further hazard lying ahead. The reason the hole is called Quarry is because of a large chasm hidden from view for first-time players on this course at about 80 yards short of the green. I use the word 'chasm' because that literally is what it is and any ball inside it is either lost or most likely will have an unplayable lie.

There are some interesting holes on the home nine which plays more inland and partly alongside a railway line that runs through the middle of the course. Perhaps the only disappointment was the 18th, a par 3 of 188 yards. An older course guide indicates that this hole was 230 yards in length so it may be that the hole was shortened possibly due to the access road to the clubhouse being not far behind the green.

As far as parkland courses go Carlyon Bay is an enjoyable round of golf with the scenery an added bonus. The compact clubhouse has great views down the course and provides very good meals in a rather different sort of atmosphere.

If you head south west on the A39 you might consider the golf course at **Falmouth**, overlooking Pendennis Point. Despite its close proximity to the sea it is not a links. There are some good holes at Falmouth, but equally the course is spoiled by some holes that are rather ordinary. When I played there some years ago one of the most interesting holes was the par 5, 8th which was 534 yards and rated the hardest. The elevated tee shot is downhill where the fairway was lined with trees as it narrows. Three trees were in a line running across the fairway and if you finished behind one of them then all you could do is play a short low half shot. I now find that for some reason this has become the seventh. They have reduced the hole to a par 4 of 430 yards and of the three trees all but the one on the left side of the fairway has been removed.

In summary it is probably worth playing but don't expect anything better than 'holiday golf'.

The final course for this adventure is **Tehidy Park** which is located just off the A30 near Portreath to the north of the town of Camborne heading to the north coast of Cornwall. The original layout was designed by local golfing identity Jim Barnes in 1922. Barnes had been the assistant professional at nearby West Cornwall and in 1916 became the inaugural winner of the USPGA. After the Second World War C K Cotton was involved and the course was substantially lengthened to 6241 yards.

 If you were starting your golfing holiday from Cornwall then Tehidy Park is not a bad place for your warm up. There are no major difficulties provided you stay on the fairway. In 1999 the club planted three thousand new trees so now the holes are tightening up somewhat and within a few more years it will be more of a wooded parkland.

 In spring and early summer you can't help but be impressed by the lovely colours of the flowering shrubs and trees. This is particularly evident at the short par 3, 7th. It is a mere 136 yards but the fairway is very narrow and it felt like you were playing in someone's backyard with all the flowers and blooms distracting you from the job at hand.

The course is generally only gently undulating with the exception of the 443 yard par 4, 15th rated Index 1. Probably the pick of the holes is the 17th, a par 3 of 193 yards over a series of ponds. The carry required is 175 yards. Anything short will find water and anything pulled a little left is likely to hit trees. On this side there are also three bunkers and at the right edge of the green is a grassy hollow and one bunker.

An unusual feature here is that OOB exists on nine of the holes. If you want a break from the seaside links then you should enjoy the easy walking Tehidy Park.

This completes the adventure through over 71 inland, parkland and heathland courses that started at North Berwick East (The Glen) in Scotland.

Golf in the Heather and Gorse compliments my previous book, *Another Journey through the Links*, which reviews in depth 165 links courses in the UK and Ireland so the two books together should help you when choosing your golf in any part of the UK.

Par 3, 17th at Tehidy Park (Photo courtesy Tehidy Park GC)

ACKNOWLEDGEMENTS

I must begin by expressing my gratitude to Peter Thomson who has now written Forewords to all five of my books to date.

Thanks to all the club secretaries who assisted with tee times and, in some cases, with photos.

As always, I had help from my dear friend in Glasgow – Duncan Martin.

Thanks also to Michael Hughes who helped organise games at Sunningdale and Swinley Forest and to Ken Macpherson who was such a gracious host at Walton Heath and who alerted me to the joys of Reigate Heath.

PHOTO ACCREDITATIONS

All photos taken by David Worley with the exception of those listed below

North Berwick East – Ian Gust

Longniddry – Glyn Satterley/Longniddry GC

Glenbervie – Glenbervie GC

Forfar – Forfar GC

Edzell – Edzell GC

Downfield – Downfield GC

Auchterarder – Archie Dunn/Auchterarder GC

Blairgowrie – Donald Ford Images

Pitlochry – Pitlochry GC

Elgin – Elgin GC

Dunblane New – Val Saville/Dunblane New GC

Callander – Callander GC

Belleisle – Paul Walker Images

Portpatrick – Portpatrick GC

Sherwood Forest – Sherwood Forest GC

Whiting Bay – Whiting Bay GC

Shiskine – Hamish Bannatyne

Moortown – Bob Seaton

Lindrick – Julian Maturi/Lindrick GC

Broadstone – David Morgan/Broadstone GC

Swinley Forest – Ben Jarvis

East Devon – East Devon GC

China Fleet – China Fleet Country Club

St Mellion – St Mellion International Resort

Carlyon Bay – Brend Hotels

Tehidy Park – Tehidy Park GC